Contents

CW00370263

Cover photographs.

Front: Striking shoemakers and their families with the Eyam Variety Players in white uniforms.
Inside Front: Strike parade, Stoney Middleton. The young woman in the middle, just to the right of the tall band member with the bowler hat, is Bertha Barber. The man on the raised bank, 3rd from the right, is believed to be Henry Hancock.
Back: Strikers and their families at one of the early strike parades. John Buckle is in the centre, with his bowler hat; Harry Dawson is just to his left, with the flat cap. Harry's daughter, Doris is one of the children on the left. The parades were vibrant community events.

Preface

I was sitting in my Grandmother's living room, soaking up the warmth of the open wood fire only half as much as the loving hospitality bestowed on all visitors to the first cottage on the right along Upper Burch Row, when 'Nan' Rose McGuinness started telling me about the book 'Tunes on a Penny Whistle.'

The book's author, Doris Coates was well known around these parts. Her first book, 'Tuppenny Rice and Treacle' had already whetted the appetite of people wanting to know about days gone by in and around her home in Eyam, Derbyshire. The village is well known for its plague of 1666, as well as being an attractive place to visit in the heart of the Peak District National Park.

I took my copy of the book home and read it in its entirety, unusual for me as I have never been one for reading whole books, even in snippets. I had been visiting Nan's Cottage in Eyam for over twenty years since our family came together again in the early 1970s. Yet I was to learn more about life in Eyam in this book than in all my previous visits, as I found a connection and resonance with the stories Doris tells.

The book contains the story of the strike that took place in the shoe factories in Eyam and Stoney Middleton around the time of the First World War. Through knowledge of her father's involvement, Doris describes the work of the trade union which sought to improve the workers' conditions and then solve what became a bitter dispute. I had never known any of this and my Nan had certainly not told me about the events of the day. However, she came to Eyam from Birchover and probably did not know herself. If she had I am sure she would have told me, as from the age of eleven I had been trained as a shoemaker and was at the time a shop steward for the National Union of Public Employees where I was then working at the Royal National Orthopaedic Hospital in Stanmore.

It was not until I moved home and work to the Peak District that the significance of the strike and the stories embroidered around it became something I wanted to research and retell. It was, after all, soon to be the hundredth anniversary of those events. It was then I met Steve Bond, who had also been doing research on the strike. We were put in touch by the late John Beck of Eyam Museum. This book, along with two exhibitions, are a part of the outcome of the research and the work we did with the local communities to commemorate the strike centenary.

Together with teams from Eyam Museum, the Stoney Middleton Heritage Group, and other residents, we've been able to bring the story back to life again. People from the two villages came together again as one to organise a variety of inspiring events. Doing the research and writing has assisted our understanding of how, even in difficult circumstances, actions started by small groups of people can bring communities together and challenge what was described as 'the old ways of doing things'.

Philip Taylor

Introduction

The strike by boot and shoemakers in Eyam and Stoney Middleton from 1918 to 1920 was remarkable in several respects. Lasting for nearly two and a half years, it was, as far as we know the longest ever strike in England in the footwear industry, and one of, if not the longest involving a group of women workers in any industry. This all took place in a rural area where trade unionism was not well established.

> A 'strike school' was set up in the village of Burston in Norfolk in 1914, following the dismissal of teachers Kitty and Tom Higdon from the local school. They were kind to the children and were principled Christian socialists – too radical for the local Rector and school managers. The children, supported by most parents protested about the dismissals, and went on strike. The Higdons taught at the 'strike school' for 25 years, supported by trade unions and individual donations!
>
> Apart from the boot and shoemakers, the longest strike by a group of women workers in Britain we are aware of was at the Grunwick film processing factory in North London. It started in August 1976 and was officially ended in July 1978.

The strike started during the First World War when agreements and laws were in place to prevent strikes and lock outs. There were attempts to seek arbitration by the Ministry of Labour at the request of NUBSO (National Union of Boot and Shoe Operatives), the trade union involved, an offer of mediation by a local magistrate, and appeals to the consciences of employers by a local vicar. None of these were successful. The dispute also involved striking workers setting up their own factory to be run on co-operative lines, and bands playing all kinds of music on strike parades!

Drawing on original archive documents, newspaper reports, trade union records, first-hand contemporary accounts of work and life, and memories passed down through generations, we have tried to give the story the recognition it deserves. It has also been our good fortune to have access to some extraordinary photographs from the period which help to bring the events and the people to life.

One of our main aims has been to bring the story alive for younger people today. School children have been able to find out more about how boots and shoes were made and how earlier generations in the villages (including in some cases their own ancestors) tried to improve working conditions and gain a voice in how they lived their lives.

Most of the strikers had left school at the age of 12 or 13 and started work straight away, but using their newfound literacy and numeracy, further self-education, and with the help of local chapels, many individuals became more confident, aware and skilled. They were no longer prepared just to accept 'the old order of things' (as trade union organizer, John Buckle put it). They ran friendly societies, music groups and religious activities, helped their neighbours, joined trade unions and political parties, and introduced their children to the delights and mysteries of the local countryside. Much of this history has been forgotten or put to one side as older generations have died, some of their children have moved away, and new people have come to the villages without knowing much of what came before.

Finding out about events like the strike can give us a different view from the more tourist inspired image of the Peak District today. When current residents and younger people in the area take action over things they feel strongly about, such as the local environment, education, housing or transport, there's a local, 'grassroots' history they can draw on.

We start with some background to the strike, looking at what life was like for people living in Eyam and Stoney Middleton in the early years of the 20th century. We then explore the nature of the boot and shoe trade in the two villages. Why did Eyam and Stoney become such significant producers of footwear? How many factories were there and who owned them? What were they like to work in?

We focus on the strike itself, why it started and then carried on for so long. Along the way we delve into the as yet untold story of the factory set up by the union and the strikers themselves. Why was it established and how did it fare?

We look at the end of the strike and consider its legacy for those involved and for the later history of the footwear trade in the area. We've made use of the wonderful oral history archive held by Eyam Museum.

We look back at the events organized for the 100th anniversary of the start of the strike and consider what a 'living history' can look like. The book goes on to describe how boot and shoemaking continues in the area and is still very much a living and vibrant trade.

Near the end, we list all the local members of the boot and shoemakers' union whom we've been able to trace from the time of the strike. We think it's important to record and remember the names of the people involved and recognise what they achieved.

We have tried to look at the strike from the perspectives of the time, rather than with today's hindsight. However, we also argue that the strikers achieved much more than they might have thought when the strike was called off in 1920. This became especially apparent during the Second World War, when boots and shoes were again in high demand and trade unions re-established themselves in the local factories.

Like Phil, I was inspired to do my research after reading Doris Coates's wonderful account of growing up in Eyam, 'Tunes on a Penny Whistle'. Doris was a child during the First World War and the strike but had vivid memories of life in Eyam at that time. Her Father, Harry worked in one of the shoe factories and was sacked in 1918 despite over 30 years service in the company and not even being in a trade union. He soon joined NUBSO however, and became prominent in the strike, chairing meetings and leading the local variety entertainers as they provided music for strike parades and fund-raising events. We'd like to thank Doris's son Richard for permission to quote from his mother's book and for republishing the book in time for the centenary commemorations.

We are aware that the employers' hostile attitude towards trade unions, and the strike itself created tensions and differences of opinion in the villages. Whilst most of the workers joined the union and supported the strike, a minority did not. There were also different attitudes amongst the local men who survived the war and came back to Eyam and Stoney

Middleton. Some supported the strike, whilst others became strike breakers. Some people were 'blacklisted' by the employers for their part in the strike and had to look for work elsewhere. It was the social divisions and potential damage to the fabric of village work and life that motivated local magistrate William Nixon to try and bring the two sides together.

There are stories which have been passed on about the events and their aftermath which draw different conclusions. We believe it's therefore especially important to try and set out the facts and the context as accurately and fairly as we can. Our book is dedicated to the strikers (about 180 of them) and their families. Their efforts paved the way for improvements at work and trades union rights for later generations. We also want to celebrate the wider and continuing contribution of local boot and shoemakers to the economy and village life over the past century.

Steve Bond

Chapter One - Turn of the century

Life in early 20th Century Eyam and Stoney Middleton was very much a story of communities trying to eke out a living from the land, local natural resources and factory work. Doris Coates, who grew up in Eyam at the time, described it as a poor village. "A few men worked in quarries and a few farmers scratched a living from the thin soil in the bleak climate," she wrote.

The nearby city of Sheffield could now be reached by train and was drawing people in from rural areas to work in the expanding steel and engineering industries. The nearest sizeable towns, like Chesterfield, Matlock and Buxton were also growing, but by 1919 were an hour's drive away when the first small motor bus started running in Eyam.

Of course, Eyam had already a story to tell, that of the Plague of 1665-66 in which surviving villagers cut themselves off from the outside world as some 260 of their community died. The people of Stoney Middleton played their part in helping Eyam by placing food in safe places around the self-imposed boundaries.

Village communities were often largely self–sufficient as the list of shops and businesses from Kelly's directory in 1912 overleaf shows. In Eyam there had also been a thriving silk weaving industry, and in both villages, there were a variety of mining and quarrying operations for miles around which provided employment. Visiting traders also offered goods not readily available in the villages.

By 1891 there were already a significant number of factories and workshops where shoes and boots were made, with a tannery in nearby Grindleford to provide leather skins. When the railway arrived for goods in 1893 (a year later for passengers), connecting the Hope Valley to Sheffield and Manchester, new opportunities arose to access markets and welcome visitors in ever increasing numbers. Boot and shoemaking replaced silk, which had relocated to Macclesfield in Cheshire, and the declining lead mining industry.

Footwear manufacture soon became a vital source of employment in the two villages. In the 1911 census, 322 people (aged 13 upwards) were recorded in the trade, about a fifth of the whole population. The total would have been higher had women employed at home on a casual basis been included.

List of shops, traders and businesses – Stoney Middleton. 1912

Boot and Shoe manufacturers (6) Bootmaker, self-employed (1)
Lime burner Blacksmith Greengrocer
Post office (note: 3 deliveries a day plus 1 on Sunday)
Conveyance Proprietor Farmers (13) Butchers (2)
Police Station Baryte (mineral) manufacturer
Drapers Wheelwright Slater
Joiner Other shopkeepers (7)
Pubs / Inns (6) Ball Inn, Stags Head, Lovers Leap Inn, Royal Oak, Grouse, The Moon.

Lord of the Manor: The Duke of Devonshire
Chief landowners: Lord Denman and the Duke of Devonshire

List of shops, traders and businesses – Eyam. 1912

Boot & Shoe manufacturers (3) Boot & Shoemakers, self-employed (3)
Blacksmiths (2) Insurance Agent Hair Dresser
Grocers (4) includes one shop which was also a drugstore and drapers
Stone merchant / Quarry owner Post Office Carpenter
Omnibus Proprietor Greengrocer Baker
Fishery keeper Spar merchant Stonemason
Tax Collector (also a farmer) Newsagent Drapers (2)
Cab proprietor (picks up from Grindleford Station) Tailor
Beer Retailers or off license (2) Farmers (17) Carter
Pubs / Inns (5) Rose & Crown, Bulls Head, Miners Arms, Foresters, The Barrel Inn.

Lord of the Manor: The Duke of Devonshire
Chief landowner: Mrs Gregory (Eyam View)

In the years before the outbreak of war, around four in ten households had at least one person working in the footwear trade, with about one third of those being women. There were three main 'shoe shops' (factories) in Eyam, and six in Stoney Middleton, though some were quite small operations. Others had been forced out of business by the development of more modern production methods in larger manufacturing centres like Leicester and Northampton.

Although not so obvious today, this was very much an industrial as well as an agricultural area. Boot and shoemaking employed most of the female labour, and a significant minority of men. Many men worked in industries such as quarrying, lead mining, lime burning and fluorspar production: and women also worked in domestic service and cotton (with a big mill nearby in Calver). There was plenty of local as well as wider demand for the work boots made in Stoney Middleton. From Eyam, shoes and slippers were sold to retailers, and for export, (especially to the empire). In the First World War, Heginbotham's in Stoney Middleton obtained contracts to make army boots, whilst Mason Brothers and Lennon undertook repairs to army boots.

Poor working conditions had a big impact on the health of many shoe workers. Tom Carter of Stoney Middleton describes how his brother-in-law, a boot finisher and former footballer, suffered from leather dust in his lungs and became ill. Frances Elliot, an active young woman and shoe worker in Eyam died from TB at the age of 21. Reports in the early 1900s showed that pulmonary TB was significantly prevalent amongst shoe and bootmakers. Harry Dawson, a 'clicker' (someone who cut the pieces of leather from a skin) at Ridgeway Brothers wrote that "there is hardly a clicker or rough cutter who hasn't lost a finger or thumb or had them crushed." The average age of death in the trade was just 44 for men and 45 for women.

Girls often had to buy candles, because their employers wouldn't light the gas, and their eyesight suffered. Typical weekly hours were 61 before the war and 59 in 1918. Wages were low. Union organiser John Buckle said conditions and pay in local factories were amongst the worst he had seen.

A group, believed to be bootmakers, outside the old Toll Bar in Stoney Middleton. (The building later became a fish and chip shop)

Education

Before the war, most children left school at the age of twelve and were often working part-time before they left, but the introduction of free state education for all children in the late nineteenth century led to significant improvements in literacy. After the war children stayed on at school till the age of 14. A variety of new opportunities for adult education were also emerging, and along with informal education through chapels and the church, this assisted the remarkable development of 'self-help' organisations like Friendly Societies and Trade Unions.

It was still the case, however, that educational opportunity remained extremely limited for working class children, especially girls. Even if a child managed to get a place in a grammar school (such as Lady Manners in Bakewell), travel from the villages was difficult, and costs of boarding were prohibitive for most families.

Eyam School in 1903

Stoney Middleton School around 1920.

Many of the young children from Eyam in the 1903 photograph (previous page) would have been working in shoe factories or serving in the army during the First World War, whilst those pictured from Stoney Middleton would probably have family members involved in strike action, or perhaps fathers who'd been in the forces, and mothers who may have become widows.

Church and Chapel

The churches too played their part in bringing the communities together and educating the children. Doris Coates points out that whilst there were significant differences between Church and Chapel, their congregations tended to come together for special occasions such as harvest festivals, Good Friday services, weddings and funerals. It was common for children to attend Sunday school at a time when attendance at church was actively encouraged by employers and membership of the churches was at a peak.

Stoney Middleton Wesleyan Reform Chapel

The Wesleyan Reform Chapel in Stoney Middleton, like many other non -conformist groups relied on lay preachers. (Tom Carter lists many of these preachers in his memoirs) Its services, and those of the chapels in Eyam were attended by many boot and shoe workers and their families. "The non-conformists were more egalitarian," said Doris Coates. The workers and small trades' people had a strong Liberal tradition in this part of Derbyshire. (Elsewhere, in the bigger English towns and cities, the political affiliation of chapel goers was often with the ethical socialism of the Independent Labour Party).

The Anglican churches, on the other hand, attracted "those who aspired to be gentry or people who doffed their caps to the gentry". Their members were more likely to vote Tory.

St Martin's Church, in Stoney Middleton (below) was therefore unusual in becoming the destination for a 'labour church parade' and service led by the Reverend John Riddlesden and the shoe operatives' trade union in 1918. (See Chapter 4)

St Martin's Church, Stoney Middleton

Families

Families and their connections to each other are important in understanding the composition of the workforce, as well as business ownership in the villages at that time. The extract shown below is from the

1911 census for Stoney Middleton showing Frederick Walton and his family. Employers often insisted that fathers bring their children, especially daughters to work as soon as they left school. Men risked losing their jobs if they didn't comply. Note both daughters are in the trade working as 'boot binders'. Marion, the youngest is only 13 years old.

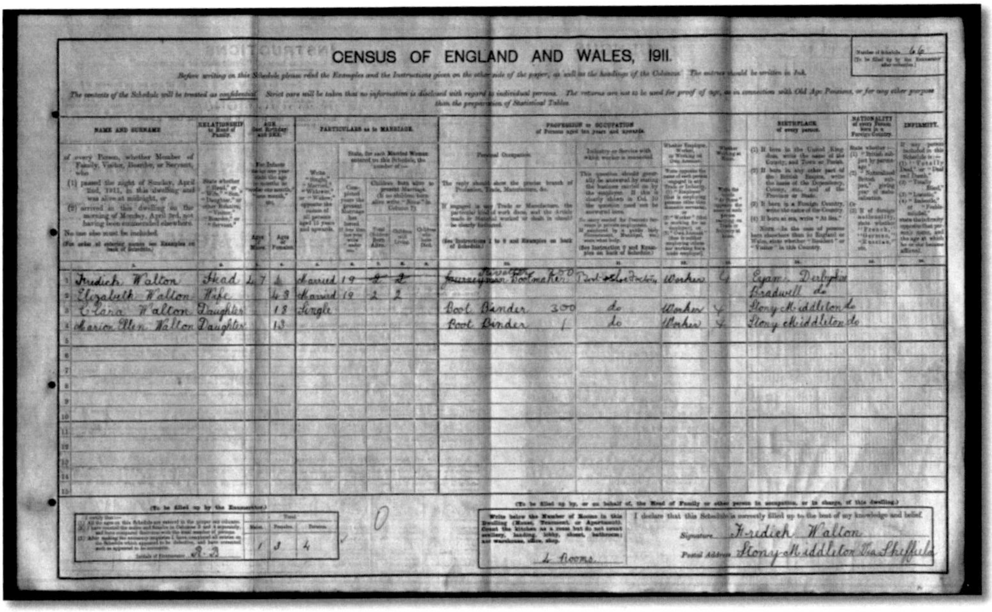

CENSUS OF ENGLAND AND WALES, 1911.

Name and Surname	Relationship to Head of Family	Age (Males)	Age (Females)	Particulars as to Marriage	Completed years the present Marriage has lasted	Children born alive	Children still living	Personal Occupation	Industry or Service	Employer, Worker or Own Account	Working at Home	Birthplace
Fredrick Walton	Head	47		Married	19	2	2	Journeyman Bootmaker	Boot Factory	Worker		Eyam Derbyshire
Elizabeth Walton	Wife		43	Married	19	2	2					Bradwell do
Clara Walton	Daughter		18	Single				Boot Binder	do	Worker		Stony Middleton do
Marion Ellen Walton	Daughter		13					Boot Binder	do	Worker		Stony Middleton do

4 Rooms

Signature: Fredick Walton

Postal Address: Stony Middleton Via Sheffield

Stoney Middleton 1911 census extract.

The second extract relates to the Barber family who came to Eyam from Manchester. Five members of the family were listed as shoe factory workers.

During the strike, family members supported each other, and members who worked in other trades could help by contributing to the family finances. There is evidence that membership of other unions, inspired by NUBSO's action was taken up by members of striking workers' families. Many of the younger men, as in the Barber family, joined the forces. Families were trying to support loved ones abroad as well as strikers on the home front.

On the employers' side too, there were connections by marriage between the various factory owning families. Members of the employers' wider families were recruited to help break the strike. Owners, like William Lennon, also had sons in the war. Correspondence he left shows how deeply he felt the pain of loss when his son Arthur died of his wounds in 1917, aged just 19.

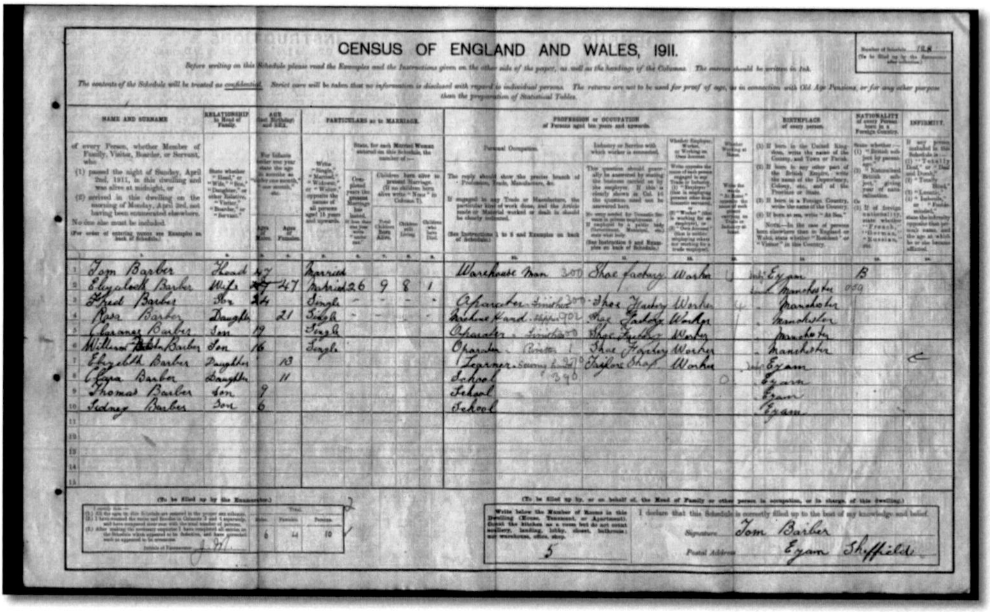

CENSUS OF ENGLAND AND WALES, 1911.

	Name and Surname	Relationship to Head of Family	Age (Males)	Age (Females)	Particulars as to Marriage	Years married	Children born alive	Children still living	Children who have died	Personal Occupation	Industry or Service	Employer, Worker or Own Account	Birthplace	Nationality
1	Tom Barber	Head	47		Married					Warehouse man	Shoe factory	Worker	Eyam	B
2	Elizabeth Barber	Wife		47	Married	26	9	8	1				Manchester	
3	Fred Barber	Son	24		Single	-	-	-	-	Operator Finisher	Shoe Factory	Worker	Manchester	
4	Rosa Barber	Daughter		21	Single	-	-	-	-	Machine Hand	Shoe Factory	Worker	Manchester	
5	Clarence Barber	Son	19		Single					Operator Finisher	Shoe Factory	Worker	Manchester	
6	William Barber	Son	16		Single					Operator Riveter	Shoe Factory	Worker	Manchester	
7	Elizabeth Barber	Daughter		13						Learner	Tailors Shop	Worker	Eyam	
8	Clara Barber	Daughter		11						School			Eyam	
9	Thomas Barber	Son	9							School			Eyam	
10	Sidney Barber	Son	6							School			Eyam	

Total: 6 Males, 4 Females, 10 Persons. Number of Rooms: 5

Signature: Tom Barber
Postal Address: Eyam Sheffield

Eyam 1911 census extract

Making Ends Meet.

Day to day household budgeting in the villages in Edwardian times was always challenging. There were few industries that paid well even for those who could venture further afield, and the slightly better off would inevitably have to share their income around their wider family. Steep price rises in the shops during the war exacerbated the problem. Ships bringing supplies across the Atlantic Ocean were attacked by German submarines. Rationing of essential items was introduced.

Government posters encouraged families to save food as more and more British troops were sent to war, and the local villages lost many of their young men to the cause. Research in Eyam for the World War exhibition at the Museum shows that over a third of the local soldiers enlisted had worked in the footwear factories.

Families involved in the strike found it especially hard. Doris Coates says her mother 'had never faced such frightening penury' and she sought domestic work in some of the bigger houses. Men collected firewood from the woods nearby, and children ran errands for coppers. 'Hot water and teas' were offered to ramblers passing through the village.

Those who had been in the union for the qualifying period received strike pay - £1 for married men, 15s for single men and 12s 6d for women. Sugar was the first item to be rationed, followed by basic foodstuffs such as flour, butter, meat, margarine and milk.

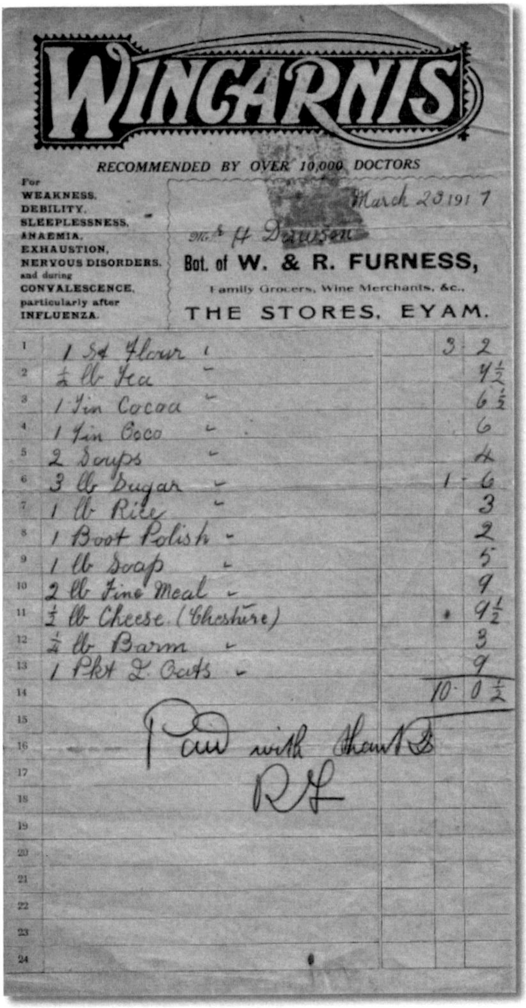
WINCARNIS

RECOMMENDED BY OVER 10,000 DOCTORS

For WEAKNESS, DEBILITY, SLEEPLESSNESS, ANAEMIA, EXHAUSTION, NERVOUS DISORDERS, and during CONVALESCENCE, particularly after INFLUENZA.

March 23 1917

Mr H Dawson

Bot. of W. & R. FURNESS,
Family Grocers, Wine Merchants, &c.,
THE STORES, EYAM.

1 St Flour	3	2
½ lb Tea		4½
1 Tin Cocoa		6½
1 Tin Coco		6
2 Soups		4
3 lb Sugar	1	6
1 lb Rice		3
1 Boot Polish		2
1 lb Soap		5
2 lb Fine Meal		9
½ lb Cheese (Cheshire)		9½
¼ lb Barm		3
1 Pkt Q. Oats		9
	10	0½

Paid with thanks
RF

Luckily, for those in need of a tonic, the Wincarnis advertised on Furness stores invoice (left) might well have helped, described as "a natural tonic incorporating herbs traditionally recognised for their ability to combat common ailments and alleviate their symptoms. It is rich in vitamins and can have beneficial effects on the circulation system and blood pressure. "

This bill from a local grocery shop in 1917 shows the importance of imports (especially from the colonies) even for a village household far from the big ports and cities. When compared with typical wages from the time (a skilled shoemaker in Eyam was only earning about 26s a week in 1917; many, especially women workers, earned much less), and bearing in mind all the other usual household expenses such as Friendly Society subscriptions, insurance, butchers, vegetables, fares, paraffin oil etc, we can see how difficult budgeting must have been.

Although rationing was lifted between the two wars, it was reintroduced in World War Two, and finally ended in April 1954 when limits to the sale and purchase of meat and bacon were lifted.

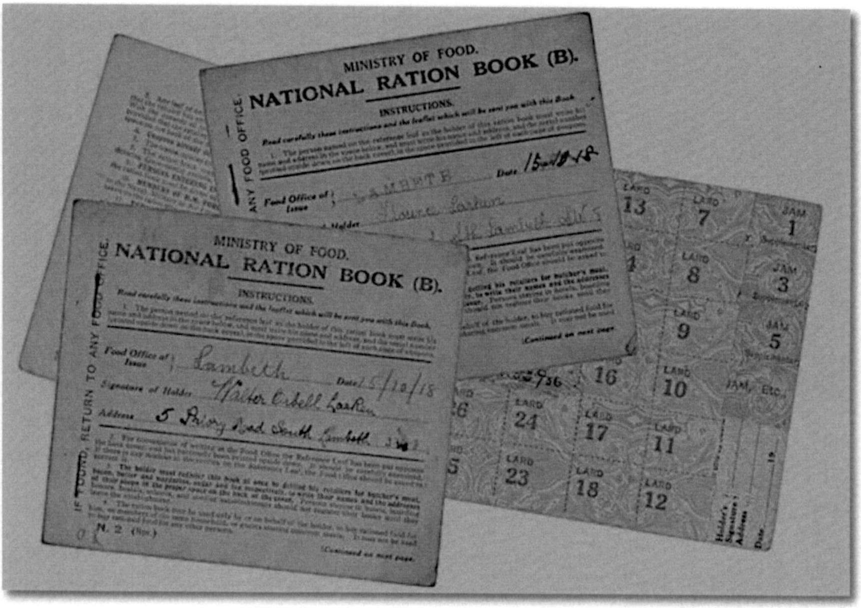

Ration books from 1918

What did people do in their leisure time?

Sports, music and other pastimes played a major role in relieving the tension and stress of the long working week and waiting for news of those men serving overseas.

Stoney Middleton football team, pictured (p19) in the grounds of the Hall (the big house), included both boot operatives and the sons of employers. Sport was a major feature of community life at the time for both women and men. Tom Carter recalls Stoney Middleton having a very good football team.

Women had been playing cricket as long ago as 1745. The Reading Mercury reported on a match that took place between Bramley and Hambledon near Guildford in Surrey. 'The greatest cricket match that was played in this part of England", the paper claimed "was on Friday, the 26th of last month, on Gosden Common, near Guildford, between eleven maids of

Bramley and eleven maids of Hambledon, all dressed in white. The girls bowled, batted, ran and catched as well as most men could do in that game'.

Stoney Middleton FC in 1913 pictured outside The Hall near St Martin's Church. The Hall was owned by Lord Denman.

Back row includes Bob Gill and Mr Shaw? Middle row includes (3) Bill Mason, (4) Mr Brightman and (5) George Ward. Front row includes (1) Teddy Barker, (3) George Unwin, (4) Tommy Hancock and (5) Percy Nugent.

Eyam Ladies cricket team, believed to be just before the war.

Stoney Middleton Royal Defence Corps 1916 *(Photo Courtesy of Ian Cox)*

People identified (not all are known)
Back row (left to right). (1) Charlie Coathan (or Cother),
(5) Wilson, (6) Mycock, (7) Barber. Middle row (1) William Lennon, (2) Joe Mason, (3) Tom Shaw, (4) Revd. Riddlesden. Front row (1) Jack Mason, (2) Worsencroft, (4) George Hall and (5) William Dawson.

The Stoney Middleton Royal Defence Corps (forerunner of the 'Home Guard') was formed in 1916. The group included employees, employers from within the boot and shoe industry as well as the Reverend John Riddlesden (middle row, sitting, second from right). Organisations like the Home Guard provided an opportunity for men over the statutory recruiting age, or who were in essential occupations, to contribute to the war effort in a quasi -military and voluntary capacity.

Strike Parade Stoney Middleton, 1918. Music was a big part of village life, with brass bands, choirs and the Eyam Variety Players (pictured above dressed in white uniforms) providing entertainment at local social evenings and on strike parades.

Local musicians

Eyam maypole dancers around 1910

Conscription.

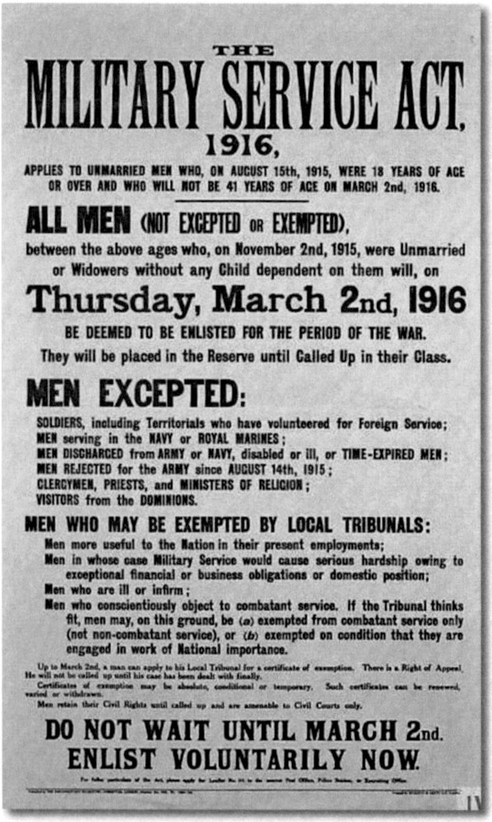

THE

MILITARY SERVICE ACT,

1916,

APPLIES TO UNMARRIED MEN WHO, ON AUGUST 15th, 1915, WERE 18 YEARS OF AGE OR OVER AND WHO WILL NOT BE 41 YEARS OF AGE ON MARCH 2nd, 1916.

ALL MEN (NOT EXCEPTED OR EXEMPTED),

between the above ages who, on November 2nd, 1915, were Unmarried or Widowers without any Child dependent on them will, on

Thursday, March 2nd, 1916

BE DEEMED TO BE ENLISTED FOR THE PERIOD OF THE WAR.

They will be placed in the Reserve until Called Up in their Class.

MEN EXCEPTED:

SOLDIERS, including Territorials who have volunteered for Foreign Service;
MEN serving in the NAVY or ROYAL MARINES;
MEN DISCHARGED from ARMY or NAVY, disabled or ill, or TIME-EXPIRED MEN;
MEN REJECTED for the ARMY since AUGUST 14th, 1915;
CLERGYMEN, PRIESTS, and MINISTERS OF RELIGION;
VISITORS from the DOMINIONS.

MEN WHO MAY BE EXEMPTED BY LOCAL TRIBUNALS:

Men more useful to the Nation in their present employments;
Men in whose case Military Service would cause serious hardship owing to exceptional financial or business obligations or domestic position;
Men who are ill or infirm;
Men who conscientiously object to combatant service. If the Tribunal thinks fit, men may, on this ground, be (a) exempted from combatant service only (not non-combatant service), or (b) exempted on condition that they are engaged in work of National importance.

Up to March 2nd, a man can apply to his Local Tribunal for a certificate of exemption. There is a Right of Appeal. He will not be called up until his case has been dealt with finally.

Certificates of exemption may be absolute, conditional or temporary. Such certificates can be renewed, varied or withdrawn.

Men retain their Civil Rights until called up and are amenable to Civil Courts only.

DO NOT WAIT UNTIL MARCH 2nd.
ENLIST VOLUNTARILY NOW.

Conscription was started in 1916 to boost numbers in the armed forces. Exemption from conscription could be claimed on specified grounds such as usefulness of occupation or conscientious objection.

Local employers put in exemption claims at tribunals for employees they wished to retain. However, when workers started to join NUBSO, some employers said they wouldn't seek exemption for union members. It would be up to individuals to pursue claims for themselves.

23 young men from Eyam alone lost their lives during World War One, and another 18 from Stoney Middleton.

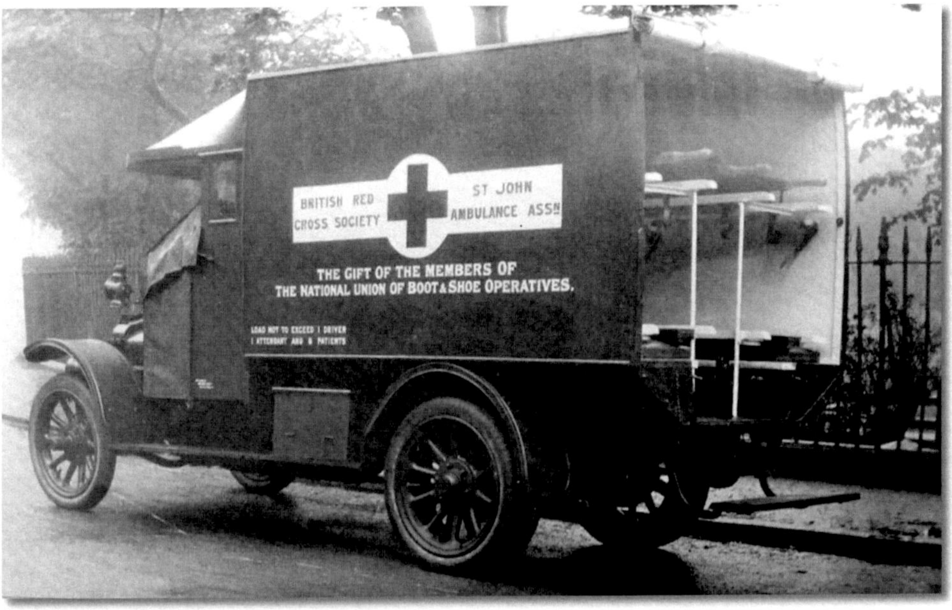

This ambulance was given to the Red Cross by NUBSO.

Poster used to persuade men to join the forces.

Chapter Two – The factories and their owners

In the late 1800s and early 1900s there were around a dozen footwear factories at different times in Eyam and Stoney Middleton as well as several smaller workshops or one-man businesses. Only William Lennon & Co. in Stoney Middleton survived into the 21st century, and the firm is still going strong at the time of writing. Many of the businesses started as small family 'cottage industries' and changed over the years, responding to the increased demand for shoes and work boots. Some firms moved into older industrial buildings previously used for such trades as cotton and silk, in one case a former corn mill, and in another, a former school. There was also a tannery nearby in Grindleford which could supply leather. The availability of skilled workers used to factory conditions was a key factor. The limited scope of other employment opportunities and the difficulties of travel also meant that employers could take advantage of relatively cheap labour.

In Eyam, the factories were mainly involved in the manufacture of shoes and slippers, lighter work in general than the heavier boots more commonly made in Stoney Middleton. There were around 200 people employed in the trade in Eyam in the mid-nineteenth century, according to one account (Wood). This number increased to around 250 at the turn of the century. Numbers fluctuated, as some firms closed, and new ones opened. The industry across the country was expanding and modernising in the Edwardian period, but this also meant greater competition for the local companies.

Stoney Middleton and Eyam were becoming recognised as a significant part of the footwear trade in the region, but wages and conditions were much poorer than in many other footwear manufacturing areas, which is perhaps why a local press report described the firms as a 'thorn in the flesh' of the large manufacturers. *(Derbyshire Times 2nd March 1918)*

The coming of the railway to the Hope Valley following the opening of the Totley Tunnel in 1893, together with the developing mechanization of the industry, put the firms in a stronger position. Supplies could arrive by train and finished goods could be sent by rail to London, Manchester and other northern cities, although road transport remained important. Mechanisation enabled higher levels and speed of production, though the firms still depended on steam power until the introduction of gas, and also paraffin engines which were introduced in the 1910s. Electricity didn't come to the villages until the 1930s. The factories were also able to put out work on a casual basis to women in local villages at times of heavy demand, a practice known locally as 'felling'.

Attempts at unionisation, in 1912 and 1916 were met with employer hostility, and there are reports of workers being suspended from employment in 1912 for joining a union.

Employers were influential in the villages, for both economic and social reasons. The boot and shoe firms were an important part of the local economy in the Edwardian period. But individual company owners also took on roles in the local community, such as being a Parish Councillor, making Church appointments, becoming a board member on a housing trust, or a Foreman of an Inquest jury. Some were also landowners and landlords of rented housing. A letter to a local newspaper gives a sense of what this might mean for their employees:

".....those who know the employers...know that their deep rooted objection to a trade union is because it means an end to their autocratic powers and an end to victimisation of any of their operatives who dare to cross their wishes either in the factory, the club room, the institute or in social or parochial life" (extracts from a Letter to the 'Derbyshire Courier' 25th Feb 1919)

Main companies

(Note: We start with the eight firms we believe were directly involved in the dispute. We then list others we have found out about. The list of firms is not an exhaustive one but gives an indication of the changing names and fluctuations in the local trade, and the significance of the industry in the two villages).

Stoney Middleton

"Why man, they've made shoes in near every house in Middleton" (Local employer Jim Goddard, speaking to Tom Carter - quoted in Carter's memoirs)

Boot and shoemaking in Stoney Middleton goes back to the late 18th century and the trade became well established over the next 100 years. This was especially in response to the demand for work boots from a range of local industries like quarrying, lead mining and farming, and from workers in foundries and factories in nearby towns and cities such as Sheffield and Chesterfield.

Cocker's

Frederick and Clara Cocker's factory was located on the Fold, just above the Chapel, until a fire in 1938 forced the company out of business. The business was originally started by Ezra Cocker who employed many of his large family, but the company was taken over by Fred and Clara when the original business failed.

In the 1890s Cockers advertised ankle straps and bar shoes, still common styles of footwear in modern times. It is believed they also made boots in the early 20th century (Tom Carter refers to 'Ezra Cocker's boot factory' in his memoirs). At different times the Cocker family had buildings on both sides of The Fold, both later becoming garages. One was owned by Claude Middleton and the other by Arthur White.

Goddard's

James Goddard's Stoney Middleton factory was located on the Bank,

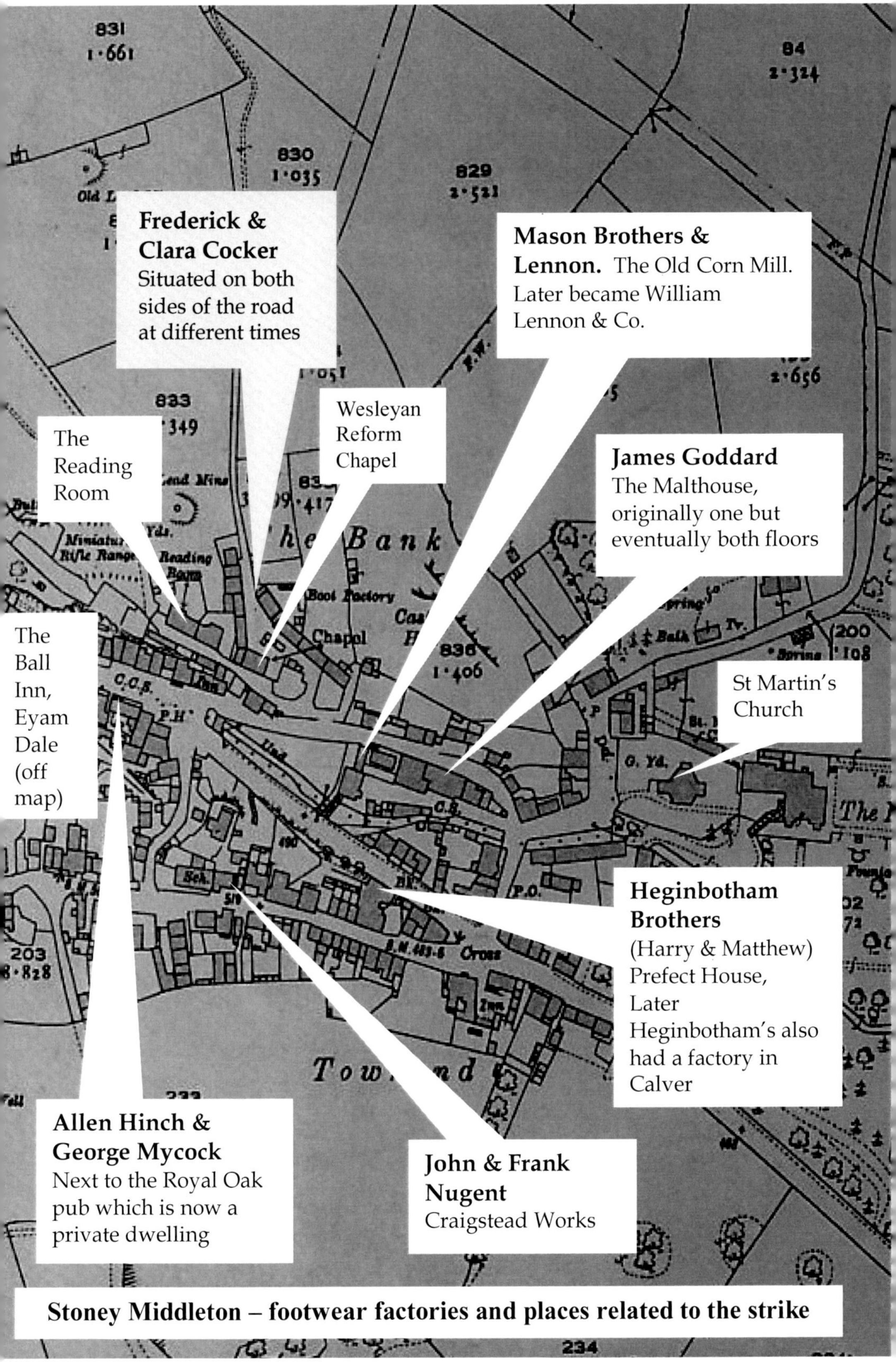

Stoney Middleton – footwear factories and places related to the strike

Goddard's moved to the top storey of the Malthouse. (At the time of writing, the building is still there, now converted to flats. Picture on p26). Tom Carter describes going to work there in the 1890s and remembering it as "one long room with the machine room partitioned off. At the top end was the press, then the riveting benches, then the finishers, then the clickers and machinists. The benching and finishing was all done by hand."

Another storey was acquired so that by 1917, this was a 2-storey operation. Tom Carter went back to work there in 1917, having been directed to do so as a 'substitute' for employees who were in the forces. The firm didn't recognize the union and was involved in the dispute during 1918-20. It is believed that William Lennon bought the building from a Mr Heppenstall but didn't take over the firm.

Heginbotham's

Prefect House Works, Main Road (The Avenue), Stoney Middleton

Joseph Heginbotham, and his son Luther set up a boot factory in a new brick building ('Craigstead') on the High Street in Stoney Middleton around 1896/7, (next to a house of the same name) Two other sons, Harry and

Matthew established Heginbotham Bros. in what is now 'Prefect House', backing onto the main road where the hoist can still be seen. A fire in 1905 reduced the building from 3 floors to 2 floors.

The Craigstead venture failed to prosper and Luther moved to Liverpool, the factory being taken over by Nugent's. Joseph worked for his sons at Heginbotham Brothers. They successfully bid for war contracts for army boots. (Recorded in the *Labour Gazette,* 1916.)

Firms delivering war contracts were supposed to adhere to nationally agreed wages and conditions. NUBSO sent John Buckle to Stoney Middleton in 1916 to try and make sure Heginbotham's were complying. The company agreed to talk to the union and to raise wages but said they would only reduce hours if instructed to do so. Buckle was pleased to get the pay rise for the employees, but disappointed that none of them joined the union.

When Buckle came back 2 years later, the union got a much more favourable response. (*see chapter four*) Heginbotham's was the only firm prepared to deal with the union in 1918 and try to settle the strike.

Craigstead Works, High Street, Stoney Middleton

Henry Heginbotham made a telling remark at the Bakewell Tribunal (which heard cases for exemption from conscription). When asked by a tribunal member what was behind the dispute, he said "It's prejudice more than anything." (The '*Derbyshire Courier*' didn't give more details, but it's likely that he was referring to the attitude of other employers, who had refused to meet the union)

In 1920, a new company, Heginbotham Brothers was established, with a capital of £10,000 and the firm set up a factory at Calver crossroads around 1923. In the 1980s, the building was converted for use as a shop for footwear and outdoor clothing. Heginbotham's become well known for developing a safety boot with steel toe caps on the outside, used in such industries as quarrying. There is a telling story about the invention. A reliable and trusted employee was adept at coming up with new boot designs. The story goes that this employee first developed the idea, but that Henry Heginbotham saw the potential and took over the project as his own. The individual was involved in the project no further, nor was he given the recognition he deserved.

Hinch and Mycock

The Royal Oak, Stoney Middleton, next to Hinch and Mycock's factory

Cousins Allen Hinch and George Mycock had both worked at Goddard's. They set up their company next to the Royal Oak pub in the Dale Bottom. Allen was said to be a good businessman but died suddenly when only 40 years old. Philip Mycock and Alfred Wilson of Curbar set up a footwear business in the original building, which is now demolished. George Mycock went up the road and established a small firm in the Old Smithy premises, (later known as The Old Studio) which continued until his retirement.

Mason Brothers and Lennon, later Wm. Lennon and Co.

William Anthony Lennon (left) founded his business in Stoney Middleton in 1899. He came to the village from Manchester as an orphan and was apprenticed to Joseph Heginbotham (see above). He also lived with the family.

William married Charlotte Goddard (daughter of quarry owner, Henry Goddard). He formed a partnership with Joseph and Gilbert Mason in 1899, repairing and later making boots in a Cottage on Dale Mouth. They moved to the Old Corn Mill (overlooking the main road) in 1903, according to records found in the factory, paying a rent of £3 5s a quarter. The partnership broke up in 1918, but William Lennon continued the business, buying the premises in 1925. A Paraffin engine was installed in 1912, and electricity 20 years later.

This was very much a family business - William and Charlotte had 9 children and most of them were involved in one way or another with the success of the firm. Sadly, one son William died at a young age of an epileptic fit, and another, Arthur was killed in the First World War. His name is on the Memorial Stone in St Martin's Church yard.

Lennon's was badly affected by both the war and the strike, though why William Lennon didn't follow his near neighbour Heginbotham Brothers' example and settle with the union is unclear. Lennon's was repairing army boots whilst Heginbotham's was making them. Both employers and employees would have known each other.

William had two sons in the army, and after Arthur's death, was desperate to get his other son, Percy, demobilised to help with the firm.

He had to close the factory for 6 months in 1918/19, as half of his workers had joined the forces, and the remaining staff went on strike.

The Old Corn Mill in Stoney Middleton, later to become the Mason Brothers and Lennon boot factory. *(Photo Courtesy of Jim Key)*

Lennon's did eventually recover and was one of the four bigger firms in the area which survived the 1930s and sought to meet increased demand during World War Two.

The company continued as a family firm, with the fourth generation taking the company past the centenary of the First World War. At the time of writing, Wm. Lennon's is the only one of the original eight firms involved in the 1918 dispute still in business, and they've stayed in the same building, though it's been extended. (See map and later chapter)

In Stoney Middleton other company names recorded in directories are William Boam Mason; George Carter; Ezra Cocker; Goddard and Heginbotham; Archilaus Hancock; Luther Heginbotham; Gilbert Mason and Son, and Charles William Payne.

Main Firms - Eyam

Two companies emerged as the main employers and producers in the village - Edmund West & Sons, and Ridgeway Brothers. They invested in new machinery and were said to be as well-equipped as many firms in the better recognised footwear producing areas such as Northampton and Norwich. They had also developed an export trade. (The *'Shoe & Leather Record'* ran a special feature on the North in 1898 and featured the two companies as up and coming manufacturers)

Ridgeway Brothers

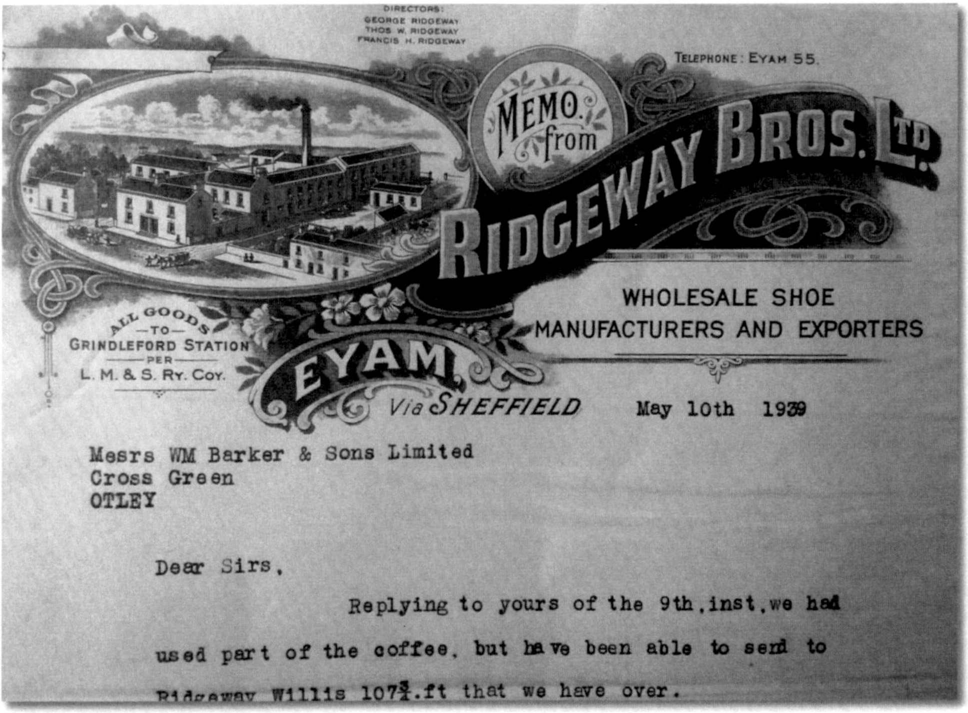
DIRECTORS:
GEORGE RIDGEWAY
THOS W. RIDGEWAY
FRANCIS H. RIDGEWAY

TELEPHONE: EYAM 55.

MEMO. from RIDGEWAY BROS. LTD.

WHOLESALE SHOE MANUFACTURERS AND EXPORTERS

ALL GOODS —TO— GRINDLEFORD STATION —PER— L. M. & S. RY. COY.

EYAM Via SHEFFIELD

May 10th 1939

Mesrs WM Barker & Sons Limited
Cross Green
OTLEY

Dear Sirs,

Replying to yours of the 9th.inst,we had used part of the coffee, but have been able to send to Ridgeway Willis $107\frac{3}{4}$.ft that we have over.

Ridgeway Brothers was founded in 1885 by the two older sons (Henry and John) of George Ridgeway, Landlord of the Bull's Head, and a farmer and shoemaker. Younger brothers Herbert and Isaac became partners in 1913 and were in charge during the war. Their factory was the Stanley Works, a substantial set of buildings just below the Mechanics Institute. The drawing of the factory on the letter head (above) gives a good idea of the scale of the works, which later became Leedums. They were probably the biggest footwear employer in the district.

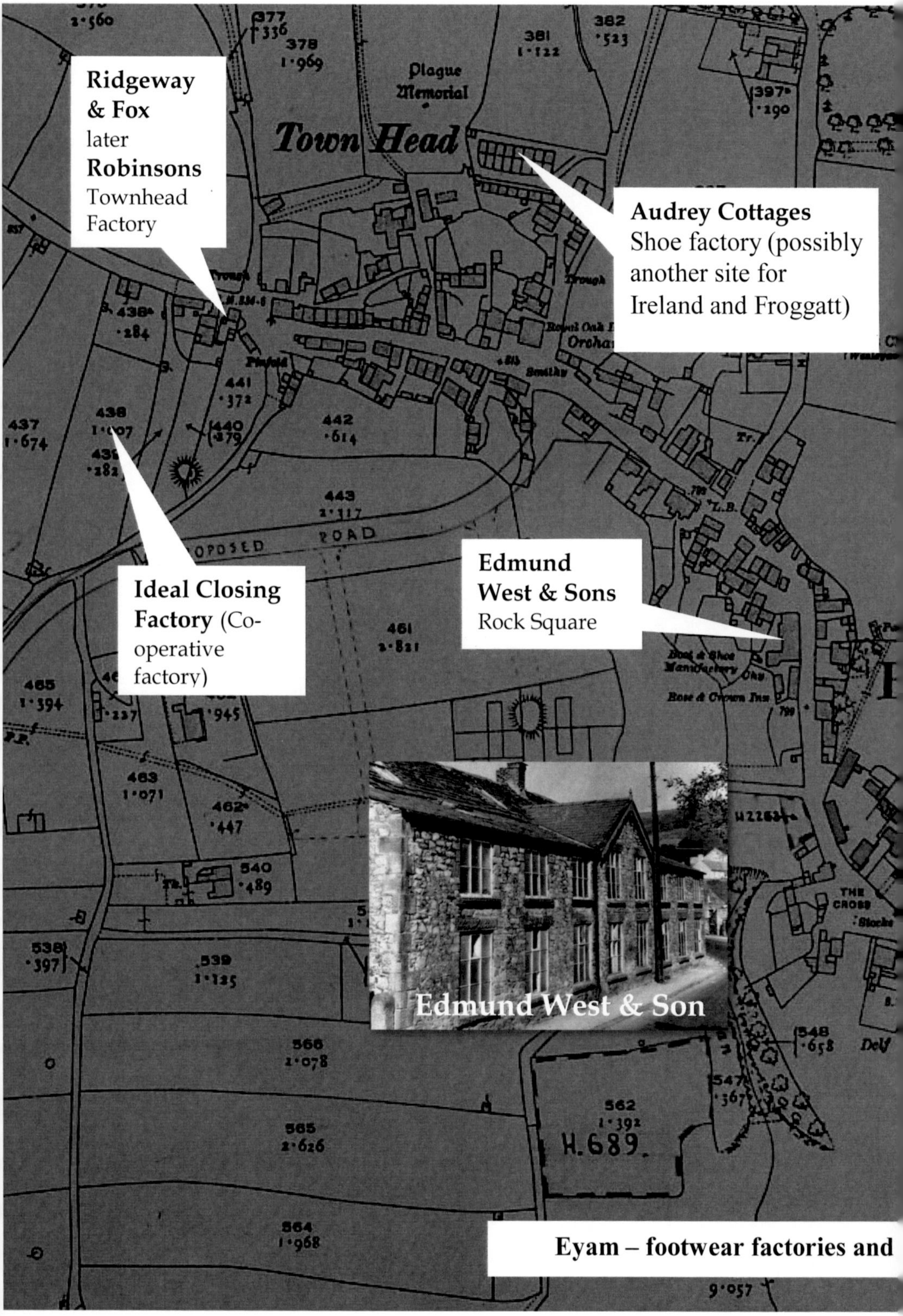
Ridgeway & Fox later Robinsons Townhead Factory
Audrey Cottages Shoe factory (possibly another site for Ireland and Froggatt)
Ideal Closing Factory (Co-operative factory)
Edmund West & Sons Rock Square
Edmund West & Son
Plague Memorial
Town Head
Boot & Shoe Manufactory
Rose & Crown Inn
THE CROSS
Stocks
Pinfold
Trough
H.689

Eyam – footwear factories and

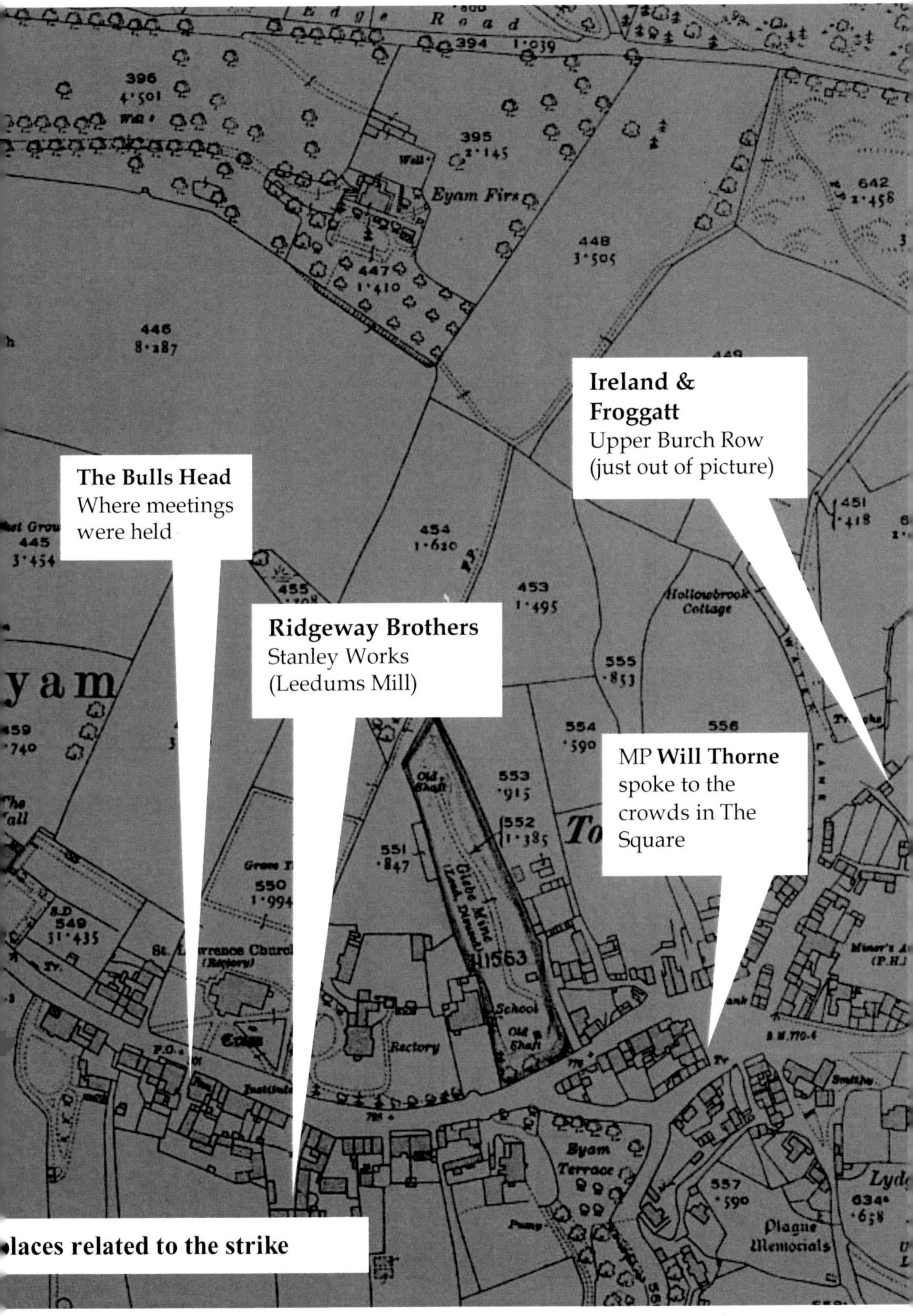

Ireland & Froggatt
Upper Burch Row (just out of picture)
The Bulls Head
Where meetings were held
Ridgeway Brothers
Stanley Works (Leedums Mill)
MP Will Thorne spoke to the crowds in The Square
Eyam Firs
Hollowbrook Cottage
School
Rectory
Plague Memorials

…laces related to the strike

When the union started recruiting in 1918 the firm sacked the NUBSO branch secretary and other workers whom they believed to be committee members. They refused to talk with the union or take part in mediation or arbitration. West's took a similarly intransigent line.

Both firms struggled to maintain production during the war, as most of their male employees either joined the forces or were on strike, along with many of the women workers, and materials were in short supply for firms which didn't have war contracts.

The Ridgeway brothers were also significant property and landowners in the village. Both Herbert and Isaac owned houses and shops, including homes rented by employees. Isaac Ridgeway, Edmund West and other employers were also Trustees on the Board which managed properties owned by the Oddfellows Friendly Society. Some of their cottages were rented by shoemakers like Harry Dawson. This became important during and after the strike, as the threat of eviction hung over workers and their families.

Isaac Ridgeway became a member of the Conservative and Unionist Party and seems to have had a political antagonism towards the union organiser, John Buckle (who later became a Labour MP), to go with his evident hostility to trade unionism.

In their correspondence with local magistrate, William Nixon, the Eyam employers particularly objected to meeting John Buckle. Nixon pointed out that Buckle didn't have to be part of the union side in any joint meetings, but apparently this cut no ice with the Ridgeways and Wests. William Nixon was himself a cutlery manufacturing employer with 60 years practical experience of trade unions. His criticism of the boot and shoe employers is therefore telling. He says to the owners that they have an erroneous view of unions if they think the unions wish to govern the employers. The risk of their rigid stance and refusal to accept mediation, in Nixon's view, is that the local trade could be ruined and the whole community might be damaged.

Ridgeway Brothers continued production after the strike, with slightly higher wages (though probably not in real terms) and shorter hours. However, they wouldn't recognise the union. In the 1930s a new set of family directors emerged, Tom, George and Francis, and for a while the firm seemed to be doing well, employing over 100 workers and exporting far and wide. However, it appears that they became over dependent on the mail order firm, Gratton's, who squeezed their profit margins. The firm was pushed into closure just before World War Two. West's bought the factory and moved its operations down the road. (*Eyam Museum Oral History, interview with Derek Knowles.)*

Herbert Ridgeway

Isaac Ridgeway with his wife Anne in a photograph taken later at a family wedding.

Edmund West

Edmund West's firm was on Church Street and Rock Square. Following demolition in the 1970s, all that was left was a wall which is now in front of a house called 'The Old Shoe Factory'.

The firm was run by Edmund and his four sons, Edmund (junior), Henry, Joseph and Phillip. Later, West's moved down the road to the Stanley Works when Ridgeway Brothers folded, and the original West's building was used by Firth's, a Sheffield steel Company during the Second World War, and later as a laboratory for Laporte Chemicals.

West's had been one of the featured firms in the *Shoe & Leather Record* supplement in 1898, noted for investing in new machinery and its exports. In the war, the firm continued production of ladies and children's shoes. It is not clear why they didn't seek contracts for war-related civilian footwear which was also in high demand. One consequence was that some materials they needed were in short supply as priority was given to war needs.

West's factory in Eyam

In 1918, Edmund West & Sons found it difficult to continue production owing to a shortage of labour arising from the war and the strike (*Shoe & Leather Record*, 7th June 1918). Most of the men were reported as being on strike. The factory workforce was apparently reduced to 8 men, 2 lads and 20 women. The firm said they couldn't find additional women workers because many had gone to work in munitions in Sheffield or to do other jobs. The company representative didn't concede that women may have been reluctant to work at West's because they supported the strikers, which was what the trade union were saying.

The Wests and Ridgeways appeared to have collaborated closely together to resist the trade union and took the leading roles amongst the local employers. (This is evident from correspondence between local magistrate, William Nixon, and the employers). Both firms dismissed employees for trade union activity. (See chapter 4)

West's survived the strike and inter war recession and picked up production during World War Two, when it also finally recognised the union.

Edmund West senior (left) died in 1920, aged 81. Edmund junior was also a director of the firm.

Ridgeway & Fox

The third of big three firms in the village at the time of the war was Ridgeway and Fox, whose factory at Townhead was once Ralph Wain's silk mill. It was also known as the 'top factory'. The mill had been converted into a shoe factory under the ownership of Knowles Brothers and Daniel. It was later taken over by Ridgeway, Fox and Slater.

Mr Slater disassociated himself from the partnership. In the 1930s the company became Ridgeway and Willis, as Mr Fox had become landlord of the Bull's Head. It was reported to be producing 1,200 pairs of shoes a week in 1932 and was featured in a Sheffield newspaper article as a thriving firm. Ironically the Bull's Head was owned at different times by two shoe manufacturers, but during the 1918-20 strike, it became the union headquarters.

Ridgeway and Fox's factory in Eyam

During World War Two, the firm was one of the four remaining large firms in the area which agreed to recognise the union and conform to nationally agreed wages and conditions. After the war, the factory was taken over by Robinsons, who moved up from Leicestershire. Some of the women who'd been at Ridgeway and Fox and joined the union in 1918 were still working there after the Second World War. Robinson's closed in the 1970s. The buildings were converted to private housing.

Other boot and shoe firms in Eyam and Stoney Middleton

Nugent's

John and Frank (Francis) Nugent moved to the Craigstead factory in Stoney Middleton after Luther Heginbotham had gone. Frank Nugent had worked for Benjamin Hallam before starting a business in a derelict house next to Verandah Cottage on the main road, just around the corner from the Moon Inn.

Nugent's were badly affected by the war and had to shut for much of the time as most of their employees had joined the forces. This was probably why they were not involved in the 1918 dispute. Nephew Percy Nugent carried on the business into the 1950s. Frank's son John was a navigator in the famous Dam Buster raid in World War Two.

Audrey Cottages

Known as the 'shop yard', previously the site had been used for a cotton factory. There was originally another row opposite the row of cottages currently standing, which was the result of a conversion of the old factory building. It is thought that at least one shoe company also used the site.

Audrey Cottages just off Little Edge, Eyam

Harry Daniel

Harry Daniel and his son Clarence ('Clarry') Daniel had a repair workshop (pictured next page) near the village square (where Curiosity Cottage now stands). Older people in the village remember congregating around the iron stove in the workshop to keep warm whilst their shoes were being mended. Clarence's private collection of around 4000 artefacts, minerals, fossils and archive documents became the inspiration for the establishment of Eyam museum which opened in 1994.

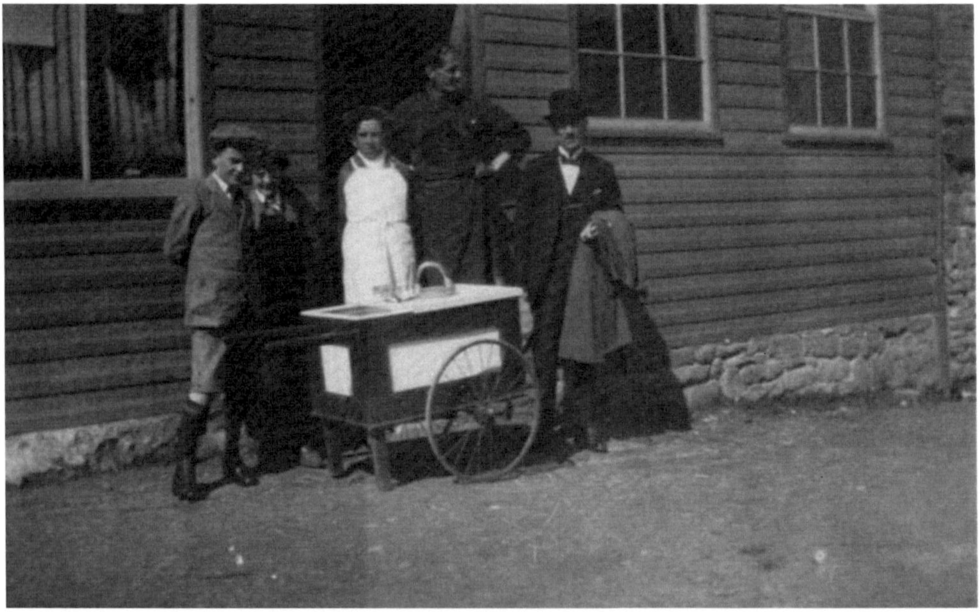

Harry and Clarence Daniel's workshop.

Ireland and Froggatt.

It is believed that Ireland & Froggatt were located at Burch Row, just off Grindleford Road in Eyam.

Hallam

Possibly the factory set up by Benjamin Hallam was the first in Stoney Middleton and used a number of derelict houses as his workshop. Benjamin Hallam had arrived as a young man from Stafford. The firm closed in the early 1900s.

Local Wesleyan preacher Tom Carter noted much of the history of the factories in his 'Cobblers Patches'.

"The first business in the village which could be referred to as a factory was begun by Benjamin Hallam. He wasn't a native, he came from Stafford.

Various empty houses were adapted and became part of his primitive factory. There seemed to be a number of hands working for him in my boyhood days. There were no Factory Acts in those days and the houses were used to full capacity".

The building to the left was once used for producing silk before becoming part of the Ridgeway and Fox shoe factory. The photograph was taken around 1935 when the factory was decorated for an employee's wedding.

Other shoe and bootmakers in Eyam listed in Kelly's Directories from 1891 to 1916 were Robert Blackwell; Samuel Sellars; Wm Bamford; Frith Brothers; Knowles Brothers and Daniel; George Young; Vincent Frith; John Daniel; James Cooper; Thomas Platts; George White; Daniel Willis; George Youle; George Young; Ben Fox; Robinson's and Harold West.

Grindleford Tannery.

Although part of the tannery was taken over by a laundry before the First World War, it did nevertheless play an important part in the development of the local footwear industry.

It is likely the tannery would have been used to process the heavier types of leathers suitable to make the work boots being made at the time. Softer 'dressed' leathers required for finer ladies and children's shoes would have required a more complex tanning process with a more skilled workforce.

The tannery became the Grindleford Model Laundry. Although not from this tannery, the photograph left gives a realistic impression of the dark and dangerous working environment that the workers would endure daily.

It is believed that there were other small tanneries in Eyam, Calver, Tideswell, Peak Forest, Hathersage and Stoney Middleton in the 1830s, in much the same ways that the shoemakers themselves were very much small family concerns and relied upon the leather tanned locally.

The area around the Hope and Derwent Valleys was ideal for the shoemaking and tanning industries. Most of the raw materials were available locally, along with a supply of cheap labour, as fewer men and women were required in the declining silk industry.

There was a ready supply of good quality cattle from the local farms, as well as good water supplies from the free-flowing waters of the Derwent River. Most of the chemicals required for the tanning processes, including locally mined lime, were also in plentiful supply.

Grindleford Model Laundry (above) closed in 2011

The laundry (and former tannery) entrance was situated in the gap between Goatscliffe Cottages, as pictured here in 1911

Chapter Three - Life in the factories, part one

"Girls who sit over sewing machines become round-shouldered and lose their eyesight by continual straining to look at the fine work before them, many times when the light is bad. One of the contemptible actions of our firm is refusing to light up the gas at early morning; or on a dull day when the girls need it".

Harry Dawson

Most people take the shoes they wear for granted in modern times. We choose to pay either as little or as much as we like depending on our budget, our sense of fashion and our desire for quality and tradition. As a result, shoes today could cost as little as a portion of fish and chips, right up to buying a complete fish and chip shop.

One hundred years ago there was far less choice. The most expensive shoes made in the local villages would only be half as much again as the least expensive. But as a proportion of earnings the difference was more profound as it would take as much as two weeks wages to provide shoes for a typical family. Old account books discovered at William Lennon's in Stoney Middleton show individual customers paying for their boots by weekly instalment ('cash on account'). So, for example, in the early 1920s there were men paying 2s a week for a pair of boots that cost 19s. (Ladies' Glace boots cost £1, and football boots were on sale for 9s)

The way shoes were made remained largely the same up until the early years of the 20th Century as rudimentary machines started to improve the productivity of the workforce, enabling the same number of operatives to increase production. It was another 30 years or so until machinery was sophisticated enough to enable employers to reduce the number of operatives required as well as improve productivity.

As electricity became more accessible and affordable, the larger shoe factories were able to utilise a range of machines that enabled them to survive when smaller businesses failed, and by the time of the Second World War nearly all production in the area centred on just four factories, West's (pictured below) and Ridgeway & Willis in Eyam, William Lennon's in Stoney Middleton, and Heginbotham's in their new factory at Calver crossroads.

Workers outside West's factory just before World War One.

The picture above is believed to be a group of shoemakers in Eyam. The young woman on the front row, 2nd left is thought to be Frances Elliott, one of the workers who joined the union in 1918.

Doris Coates's father Henry ('Harry') Dawson (pictured left with his wife Margaret and children Doris and George) described the conditions workers faced in the early 1900s. His account quoted from in Doris's book 'Tunes on a Penny Whistle' provides a rare 'workers' eye view' of what factory life was like.

Harry Dawson describes a typical day of work. "First it is necessary to go to the storeroom for the leather required. When this is produced men will cut out of the skins the various parts which comprise the upper. Much of this was done by hand with a cardboard pattern and a sharp knife. That is how they got to be called 'clickers'; they continually ran their knives along the edge of the table to sharpen them, and the great rapidity with which the knife was drawn caused it to make a clicking sound".

"After we got all the pieces of leather which comprise the uppers (and probably five or six people have cut various pieces), we take them to the binding room. Here a woman, or a young girl who is called a binder, will trim the edge of the various pieces and join them together to make up the complete uppers".

"We next take our uppers to the 'rough-cutting' room where the piece of leather which comprise the soles, insoles and heels are cut out. Heavy machinery is required for this work. Large pieces of leather are placed on a block of wood and knives of the shape of the soles and heelpieces are put on them, and by pressure of the machine chopped out of bends of leather. This work is dangerous, as persons working these machines are liable to have fingers or thumbs taken off by the machine".

"Having got the uppers and all the various pieces of leather necessary, we got to the riveting room where the soles and heel-pieces are fastened together. Here we see some wonderful machinery. Iron blocks the shape of a foot are used. The insole is tacked on, then the upper pulled over the insole, and at the same time drives in a tack to hold it in place".

"Having got our upper tacked on, the sole is then tacked on heel to toe. Then it is taken to a riveting machine, which drives in rivets round the edge of the shoe, as quick as a sewing machine makes stitches".

"All the parts which comprise the heel are placed in a groove of the size of the heel. The boot is placed with the sole down upon the heel pieces, a movable arm is placed in the boot, and a lever pressed by the foot. Rivets are forced upwards through the heel pieces, and through the sole, making it secure to the boot".

"Our boots are now made, but the edges of the soles are rough and unpolished, so we take them to the finishing room to be polished off. A machine with a circular knife, making 400 revolutions to the minute, soon smoothes the edges and the heels. After the edges have been inked or coloured, the edges and heels are polished by circular irons, the friction of which polishes the boot".

Tom Carter's memoirs, 'Cobbler's Patches of Memory' (1956), is the other local first-hand account of working in the trade 100 years ago that we've come across. It's a wonderfully detailed description of Stoney Middleton from the late nineteenth up to the mid twentieth century. Tom worked at several local boot factories and then joined his brothers in establishing their own boot making and repairing business in Calver. He was sent to work at Goddard's in 1917 to substitute for men who'd joined the forces. We believe he joined the union and the strike in 1918. Writing about the history of boot making in the village, he said:

"I think the family firm of Heginbotham's began with the father Joseph. The first workshop of theirs I remember was in one of the now demolished houses on the left-hand side of the town. Then they moved across the road to the premises which now have doors to both the town side and the New Road. A disastrous fire gutted the place, and only two stories were rebuilt". (Note: This is the factory building which can still be seen on the main road with the hoist outside. See picture on p28).

"The Craigstead Boot Factory was built by Luther Heginbotham after he and his brother Harry had dissolved their partnership. Matthew seemed to take the place of his brother Luther in the partnership".

"Fred Cocker was fortunate in one respect when he started his business, he had a large family and most of them worked in the business. The garage opposite now owned and used by Arthur White was originally built for a shoe factory and occupied by Cocker's".

Tom Carter

"They were working 59 hours a week and wages were very near the bone, with no bonus... another Eyam plague"

Union organiser John Buckle

"There was a man known as Dickie Chapman who, with his wife lived in the little house on Nettle Hill where we started our married life. I'm told he used to get the uppers and 'bottom stuff' from the factory in Eyam and make them in the kitchen end".

Tom Carter

"Meeting at Stoney Middleton in reading room. 21 males joined the union. Male operatives are making pit boots, carters' boots, navvies' boots. 9 pairs a day for 35/- per week for 58 ½ hours"

John Buckle. Jan 1918

"Meeting of female operatives at Stoney Middleton. Highest wage 16/- a week of 55 ½ hrs. No bonuses paid."

John Buckle. Jan 1918

"In the days when I first worked at Heginbotham's, the working hours were six am to six pm with half an hour allowed for breakfast and an hour for dinner. Saturdays were six a.m. to one p.m. with half an hour for breakfast......The Saturday 'knocking-off time' was reduced from one o'clock to twelve-thirty. These hours 'held good' until the middle of the 1914-18 war. Wintertime lighting was supplied by the old paraffin lamps...Wages were 24/- for men, and I think 12 /- for women. Odd men got 26/- but it seemed to be paid surreptitiously, for fear of causing discontent among the others. Boys started at 4/-a week full time."

Tom Carter

A report by Seebohm Rowntree in 1918 argued that the minimum weekly needs of an unskilled worker with a family of 3 children at 1914 prices was 35s 3d. The '*Derbyshire Courier*' noted that prices had doubled during the war so the required wage in 1918 would be much higher.
The paper quoted as an example "...the tireless struggle of those decent folk in Eyam and Stoney Middleton" who still had so far to go to earn this amount.

Rivetting

"I had always wanted to be a rivetter, and eventually.... got my desire. For the sake of speed, it was an unwritten law that all rivets, both from iron and brass had to be used from the mouth. The iron rivets were alright, but the brass ones were distasteful, and nature resented their presence.... I particularly remember what were called 'steel bills'. They looked for all the world like the 'visiting cards' of mice and were almost as nauseous. I used to have a sore throat when I used them.... The rivet boxes were mostly communal, one to about four men or lads.....Using rivets after smokers was bad enough, but odd ones among them chewed tobacco as well. That was foul. No chewer ought to have been allowed on the rivetting bench.

Overall, the men got on well together, without much bad feeling. A few rough practical jokes were inevitable, but there was always a policy of 'give and take'. Hard and constant work always kept the brake on."

Tom Carter, Cobbler's Patches, pp 166 - 168

(Note: We came across two different spellings of the term rivetter, with one and two 't' s. Tom Carter used two 't's).

Chapter four - The strike

Compared to other parts of the country "operatives in Eyam and Stoney Middleton are compelled to work longer hours for much lower wages." (*Derbyshire Courier* 2nd Feb 1918). In Leicester, where the union was strong, men were earning 75 - 100 shillings (£3.75 - £5.00) a week, compared to 36 shillings locally (£1.80). Women's wages in the local factories were "near to the bone", 12 to 16 shillings for a 58 or 59 hour week, whilst the national agreement was for 52.5 hours.

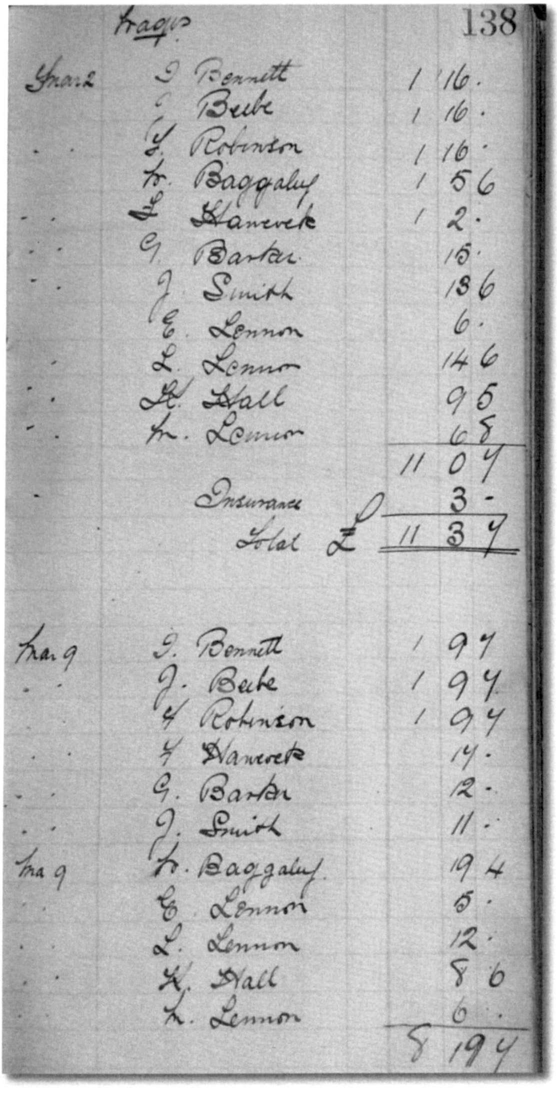

	Wages		138
Mar 2	G. Bennett	1	16 .
	C. Beebe	1	16 .
	Y. Robinson	1	16 .
	H. Baggaley	1	5 6
	L. Hancock	1	2 .
	G. Barker		15 .
	J. Smith		13 6
	E. Lennon		6 .
	L. Lennon		14 6
	H. Hall		9 5
	H. Lennon		6 8
		11	0 7
	Insurance		3 -
	Total £	11	3 7
Mar 9	G. Bennett	1	9 7
	J. Beebe	1	9 7
	Y. Robinson	1	9 7
	Y. Hancock		14 .
	G. Barker		12 .
	J. Smith		11 .
Mar 9	H. Baggaley		19 4
	E. Lennon		5 .
	L. Lennon		12 .
	H. Hall		8 6
	H. Lennon		6 .
		8	19 4

The picture to the left is an extract from Mason Brothers and Lennon's wages book for the two weeks before the strike in 1918. (Women and young workers earn between 6 and 15 shillings; the highest male wage is 36 shillings per week) Wages could also fluctuate from week to week, so there was no guarantee that workers would get the full rate all the time.

The National Union of Boot and Shoe Operatives (NUBSO) sent national organiser, John Buckle to Derbyshire. Buckle had been to Stoney Middleton and Eyam in 1916, when Heginbotham's had obtained a war office contract for Russian army boots. (Apparently, they had to produce 1200 boots a week and not take on other orders until the contract was completed). Buckle managed to persuade the firm to increase pay for men from 24s to 32s a week and increase women's pay by 5 s a week. He was less successful in recruiting union members but became convinced that it was possible to get NUBSO established in the two villages. (*Minutes of NUBSO National Council, June 1916)*

With agreements in place on war related work, and the union seeking improvements in wages and conditions nationally, it was important for the union to try and obtain recognition in all parts of the country. If some employers got away with longer hours, and paying wages below rates agreed with federated firms, they could undercut companies which were adhering to national agreements. This could threaten jobs of NUBSO members.

There was much discussion in the unions and the women's suffrage movement about how far workers should go to protect wages and conditions, when so many of their fellow citizens were away in the forces. The Government banned strikes in essential industries, and insisted on 'dilution', whereby women and semi- skilled workers could be taken on in jobs previously done by skilled male workers. But there was pressure from unions to increase wages to keep pace with rising prices, and to tackle profiteering by employers. NUBSO's attitude was that those still working were 'holding things in trust' for the absent men. On a visit to Derbyshire, Walter Smith, John Buckle's fellow union organiser, questioned why workers at home would choose to make conditions worse, whilst the soldiers were making sacrifices abroad. The union wanted to ensure that the soldiers who came back had decent jobs to go to. (*Derbyshire Courier 9th Feb 1918*) Smith also argued that the situation in Eyam and Stoney Middleton was unique. He didn't know of any other footwear industry centre where employers had refused a request by the union to meet.

A letter written about Eyam to the *Derbyshire Courier* in March 1918, made the point powerfully. The writer referred to lads who had joined the forces and used to gather in the village and talk things over "*…who have gone and done their bit,* (and) *are not coming back to the old order of things."*

John Buckle came back and started having indoor and outdoor meetings with workers in the two villages in December 1917. At the beginning of January 1918, 43 men in Eyam decided to join and set up a local union branch. Amongst the first to join were Bill Slater, who became branch secretary, Tom and Bill Barber, Farewell Barnes, Charles Bramwell and Herbert Lowe. (See chapter ten for complete list of members).

The Eyam women then held a meeting at the Bull's Head on 3rd January and 46 of them signed up with the union. They included Clara Barber, Nellie Askham, Dora and Gertrude Rowland, Louise Cooper, Rose and Beatrice Bullard. This was a crucial breakthrough because women had become the majority of the work force in the local factories during the war. Their work situation could probably be compared to the 'sweating' in trades like tailoring. Intense labour conditions, a poor working environment, low wages paid by the piece, a ready supply of labour and a lack of trade union organisation were characteristic of both factory and home working in the villages. John Buckle described the working conditions as "…another Eyam plague."

The union members were mainly younger women, older men and teenagers. Most men under 40 had either volunteered for the forces or been conscripted.

The employers' response was swift. Ridgeway Brothers in Eyam sacked the new union branch secretary, Bill Slater. The companies also declared they would no longer seek exemption from conscription for essential workers, if they joined the union.

The bootmakers in Stoney Middleton were reluctant at first to join the union, possibly because of intimidation by their employers. (A sign posted in one of the factories said "No trade unionist employed in this factory"). However, following Slater's dismissal, Buckle held further meetings at the Reading Room, and workers from the Stoney factories started joining NUBSO. The first group of members included Isaac Bennett, Alice Jackson, George Hodgkinson, Clara Walton, George Ward, Sarah Robinson and John Mason. It was decided to have just one union branch, covering workers in both villages. Bill (also known as 'Willie') Slater was taken on by the union as a paid local secretary to help recruit members and organise the branch.

Local employer hostility to the union was stark. Most footwear employers around the country recognised the union. But when NUBSO officials visited the local firms, all the owners with the later exception of

Heginbotham's, refused to talk to the union. One employer was reported as saying: "We want nowt to do wi' the union." Edmund West and Sons, the other main firm in Eyam, followed Ridgeway's example by sacking union branch president Tom Barber and his son and daughter. Ridgeway Brothers and West's between them sacked at least 11 (and possibly 13) men and women whom they believed were the main union activists. (One of them, Harry Dawson wasn't even a union member. He soon joined however and took an active role in the union and the strike.) However, the dismissals didn't have the effect the employers wanted, leading only to calls for strike action. Employers threatened to close factories if workers didn't sign documents saying they would not join the union. On Thursday 28th February, Ridgeway Brothers suspended all their employees until the following Monday, whilst West's suspended operatives in the finishing department for a week.

In February NUBSO had written to the Ministry of Labour to see if they could bring the employers into talks. On 4th March NUBSO General Secretary, Edward Poulton wrote to the Ministry again, asking them to intervene to seek a settlement. Arbitration was accepted practice in the industry, and part of the government and unions' wartime agreement. But the employers wouldn't accept there was a dispute. (See correspondence on pages 57 & 59)

The history of the National Union of Boot and Shoe Operatives can be traced back to 1873 when many riveters and finishers left the Amalgamated Association of Boot and Shoemakers after becoming dissatisfied with their low status within the old union. They formed a partnership with the clickers and rough cutters union.

NUBSO's membership grew rapidly to around 44,000 following the 'boom' of the early 1890s. However there was a set-back in 1895 following a long dispute over a minimum wage and an 'employer lockout'. Membership fell to 24,000 by 1906, but it increased again during the war with the massive demand for boots, and reached over 100,000 by 1920. NUBSO supported over 20,000 of its members who 'joined the colours' in the First World War. 2,591 of them lost their lives, and 3,685 were injured.

The Ministry of Labour contacted the employers, but Chief Commissioner Sir George Askwith's response (p59) illustrates the dilemma facing the union. If the employers refused to meet, then the Government could only insist on arbitration if war contracts were at stake. As none of the eight local companies involved had such contracts at the time, (Heginbotham's seems to have completed its army boot work), the Ministry of Labour didn't feel it could intervene. And because the local firms weren't part of the boot and shoe employers' federation, the usual industry procedures (designed to avoid strikes and lockouts) didn't apply either. Union members would have to decide whether to strike, with all the risks entailed. (*Matlock Guardian* 16th March 1918).

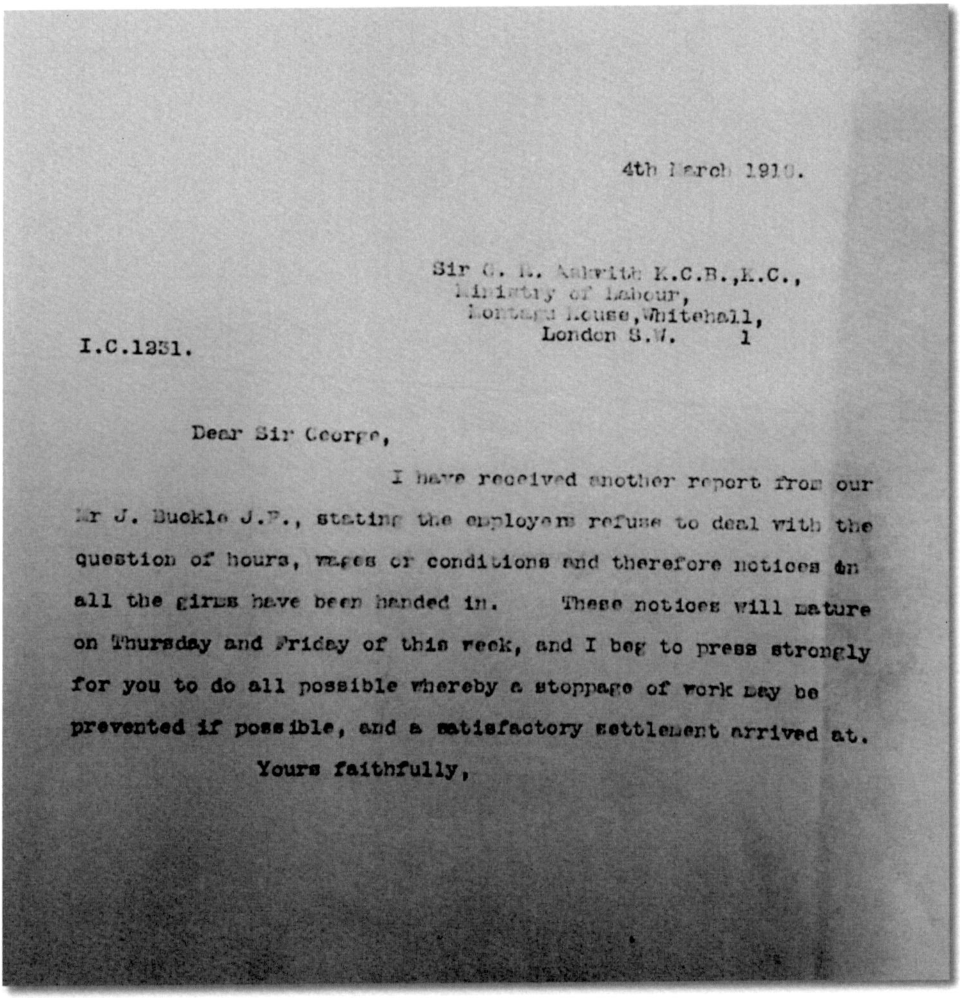

4th March 1918.

Sir G. R. Askwith K.C.B.,K.C.,
Ministry of Labour,
Montagu House, Whitehall,
London S.W. 1

I.C.1231.

Dear Sir George,

I have received another report from our Mr J. Buckle J.P., stating the employers refuse to deal with the question of hours, wages or conditions and therefore notices on all the girls have been handed in. These notices will mature on Thursday and Friday of this week, and I beg to press strongly for you to do all possible whereby a stoppage of work may be prevented if possible, and a satisfactory settlement arrived at.

Yours faithfully,

Correspondence between NUBSO and the Ministry of Labour (*Modern Records Centre, University of Warwick*)

The union was reluctant to engage in strikes, especially in war time. Buckle had persuaded his members to refrain from action until attempts at arbitration had been pursued. The Union's General Secretary, Edward Poulton visited Eyam and Stoney Middleton, and his address to public meetings was reportedly '......of the most conciliatory nature'. It was only after the employers had turned down requests to meet Poulton or other NUBSO representatives, had rejected claims from workers for shorter hours and payment of a war bonus, and also spurned the Ministry of Labour's approach, that the union confirmed it would go ahead with strike action. This entailed individual employees handing in their notice, a legal requirement at that time, prior to a strike. The strike was to start in Eyam on March 7th 1918, and at the Stoney Middleton factories the next day.

Freddy Richards, the union's National President reported in March that 137 operatives in the firms affected had initially joined the strike. (This number later went up to 160, and over the whole course of the dispute, union records show that Eyam branch had more than 180 members)

So, why did the strike take place?

- The employers sacked workers they believed were union branch committee members. This incensed the workers.
- The companies refused to accept an offer of conciliation by the Ministry of Labour.
- Employers wouldn't meet union representatives or consider workers' demands.
- Wages were low and conditions poor in comparison to other footwear manufacturing centres.
- Growing union membership across the country, especially amongst women probably encouraged workers to feel they could achieve something.

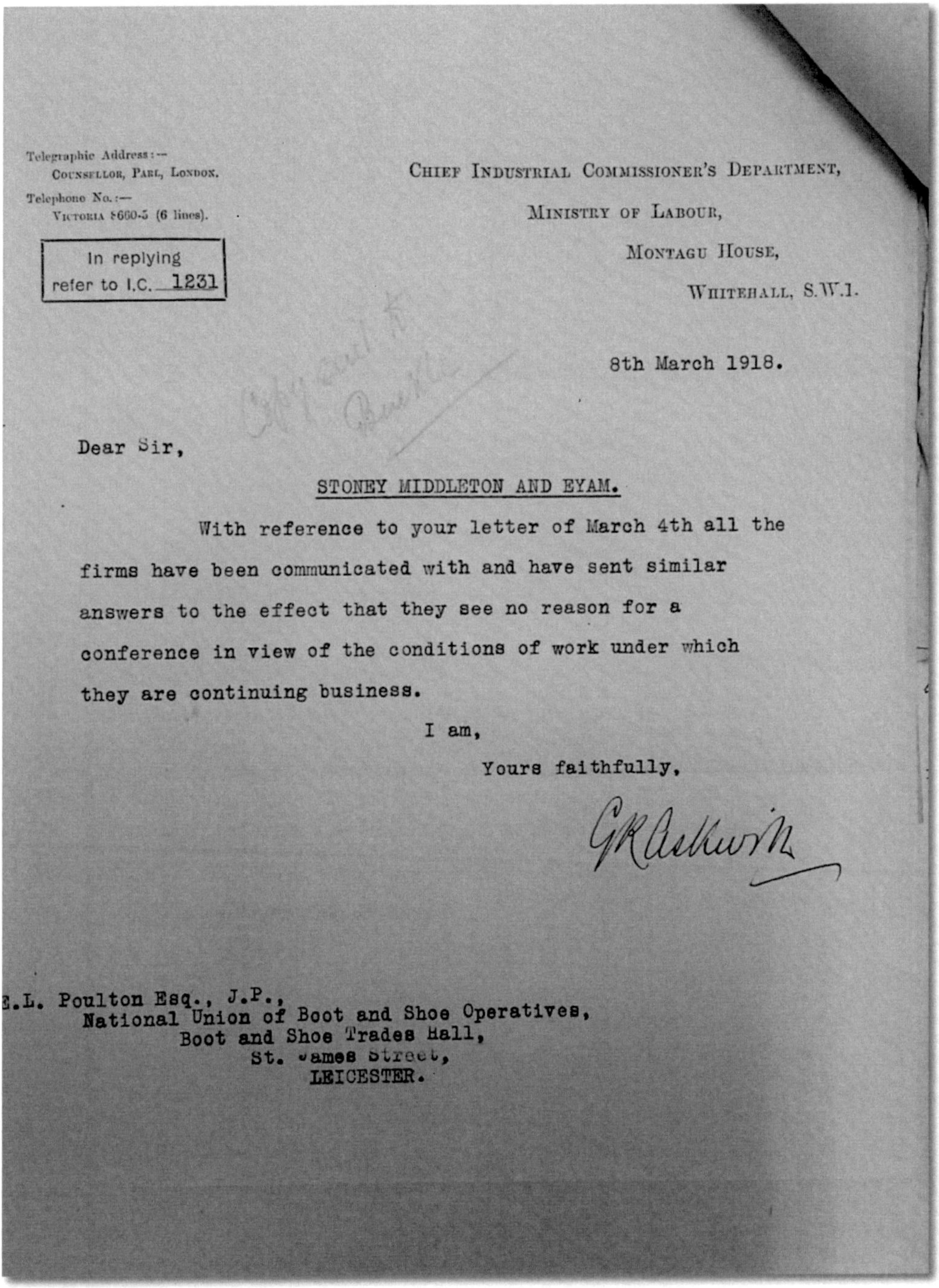
Telegraphic Address:—
COUNSELLOR, PARL, LONDON.
Telephone No.:—
VICTORIA 8660-5 (6 lines).

In replying refer to I.C. 1231

CHIEF INDUSTRIAL COMMISSIONER'S DEPARTMENT,
MINISTRY OF LABOUR,
MONTAGU HOUSE,
WHITEHALL, S.W.1.

8th March 1918.

Dear Sir,

STONEY MIDDLETON AND EYAM.

With reference to your letter of March 4th all the firms have been communicated with and have sent similar answers to the effect that they see no reason for a conference in view of the conditions of work under which they are continuing business.

I am,
Yours faithfully,
G R Askwith

E.L. Poulton Esq., J.P.,
National Union of Boot and Shoe Operatives,
Boot and Shoe Trades Hall,
St. James Street,
LEICESTER.

Reply from George Askwith at the Ministry of Labour to the union.

Once the strike had started, John Buckle used his base at the Bull's Head in Eyam as the strike headquarters and he sent out an appeal for support round the country (See p61). It's interesting to note the union's demands did not include a basic wage rise but did seek payment of a war bonus which had been agreed nationally with boot and shoe employers, as well as a shorter working week.

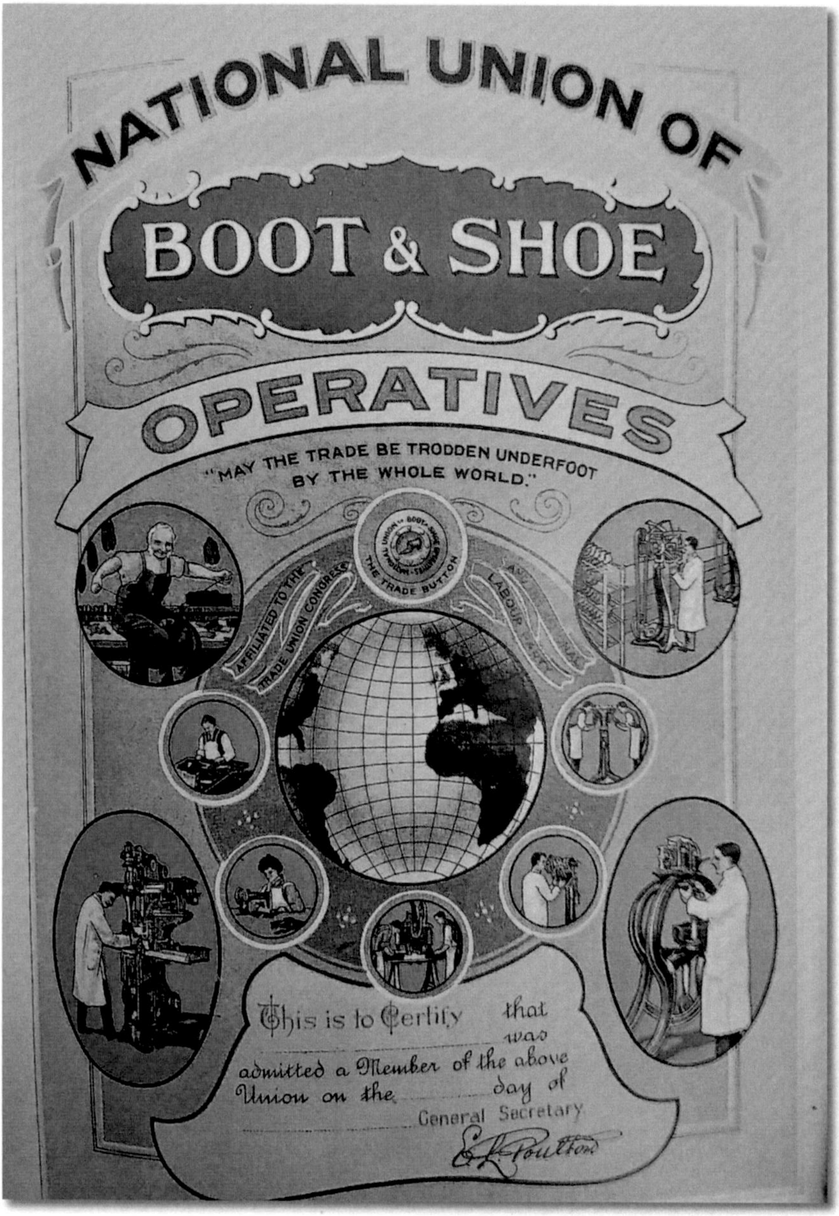

NUBSO membership certificate.

In villages like Eyam and Stoney Middleton, where employers were powerful figures in the community, joining a union was a big decision. It carried the danger of losing your job or your home.

AN APPEAL TO MEMBERS AND OFFICERS OF THE NATIONAL UNION OF BOOT & SHOE OPERATIVES.

Bull's Head,
Eyam, Derbyshire.
19. 3. 18.

Fellow Members,

For the first time since the inception of the Boot & Shoe industry, about 10 years ago, the Boot & Shoe operatives of Eyam and Stoney Middleton, two villages situated in the Peak of Derbyshire, Eyam village engaged making Ankle and Bar-Shoe work, while at the other village, Stoney Middleton, the operatives are engaged on strong work, mostly Pit Boots, and in normal times, 500 operatives will be employed at the two villages, the operatives are at present on strike, having given their notices in to the employers for the following reasons.

On Jan. 1st. 1918 it was decided after hearing an Address on Trade Unionism, by J. Buckle, J.P. Union Organiser, to form a branch of the National Union of Boot & Shoe Operatives. The officers and Committee were duly elected.

A fortnight later the Employers of Eyam set to work to stamp the new Unionism out of existence, the Branch Secretary was dismissed, this was followed by the discharge of the Branch President, his son and daughter, later other members of the Branch Committee, until there were eleven operatives "sacked" and in all cases the Employers stated reason was because the operatives had joined the Union. In spite of this harsh treatment, the operatives acted on the advice of the Union Organiser, and continued their work in the usual way, while the Union Officials were endeavouring to bring about a settlement, by methods of conciliation.

Mr. T. F. Richards, General President, Councillor W.R. Smith, Organiser, J.P. and J. Buckle J.P. Organiser, have attempted to interview the Employers at the two villages, and at each firm were refused such interview, and in every case the expression was, We shall have nothing to do with the Union. The Employers have declined the invitation of Sir George Asquith the Chief Commissioner of the Government Industrial Department, with a view to a conference being convened to talk matters over. After every method of conciliation had been tried and failed, the Operatives were very reluctantly advised to hand in their notices, The notices having expired, the operatives are now on strike.

Our demands are:-

1st. Recognition of the Union.
2nd. Reduction of hours from 59 to 52½
3rd. National War Bonus.
4th. Reinstatement of all discharged for joining the Union.

The operatives who have now been on strike for a fortnight are being financially assisted by our Union. This appeal is made to all Members and Officers of our Union, to do all that is possible by Grants, and Shop Collections to assist in this struggle. The reasons are that owing to the Operatives not having opportunities to obtain fair conditions and wages in the past, has made it impossible for them to prepare or make any provision for any such circumstance as a Strike, forced upon the operatives by the employers' attitude, and in view of the abnormal prices of the necessities of Life, this makes the struggle for the operatives with large families much harder than normal conditions would have done, and for this reason must have some additional financial assistance, in this fight against the Eyam and Stoney Middleton Employers of Labour "Whos" have refused any negotiations by representatives of our Union, also challenge the right of the operatives becoming of our Union.

Remember the brave men and women of Eyam, the village of Plague Fame in the year 1666,

All contributions forwarded to above address will be promptly acknowledged. I remain Yours faithfully,

Johnnie Buckle, Nat. Organiser.

John Buckle's appeal for support for the strikers. Recognition of the union was the key, as this could lead to negotiations on wages and other issues.

Mary Bell (left), later Bell-Richards, played a significant role in persuading women to become union members. She built up a branch of over 5000 women in Leicester and was elected onto the union's National Council.

Striking carried a high risk of workers losing their jobs, but they started in good spirits. They marched from the Eyam Mechanics Institute to Stoney Middleton with a local band on March 8th. In addition to union recognition, shorter hours and payment of the national war bonus, they wanted the reinstatement of their sacked colleagues.

The strikers organised processions which started out from Eyam Mechanics Institute (building with pillars on the left, bottom of page 63) and the Bull's Head pub (two doors to the right), the strike 'HQ'. They tried to persuade workers still in the factories to join them and looked for wider community and trade union support.

The strike parade held on March 16th was described in the *Derbyshire Times* as 'lively proceedings'. The Eyam Variety Entertainers and brass bands in both villages played an important part in the strike parades and the social life of the community.

The strike parades attracted large numbers of people including children in both Eyam and Stoney Middleton. From the press reports and photographs, they appear to have been vibrant community events.

NUBSO held meetings in the Bull's Head in Eyam and started many marches at the Mechanics Institute (with pillars, founded 1859).

(Photograph Courtesy of Jim Key).

John Buckle (left) had described Eyam in 1916 as "a little spot, off the map," but became impressed with the determination and solidarity shown by the workers who joined the union in 1918. He is also seen, wearing his bowler hat in the centre of photograph above.

One of the speakers at the early rallies was local magistrate and Eyam resident William Nixon. He sympathised with the strikers and tried to persuade the employers to enter talks. However, he also advised NUBSO members to be careful with their language and not to give the employers excuses for refusing to meet them.

On April 14th, 1918 a 'labour church parade' was organised by NUBSO in conjunction with the vicar of Stoney Middleton. Strikers and supporters marched from the Ball Inn, a pub at the junction of the road from Eyam to Stoney Middleton. They were led by a band playing 'Onward Christian Soldiers'. The Parade made its way to St Martin's Church where the

Reverend John Riddlesden preached a sermon based on the story of Cain and Abel, and its central question, 'Am I my brother's keeper?' He argued that whilst some people claimed to be their brother's keeper, they didn't live up to this in practice. "The labourer is worth his salt" Riddlesden said, and he hoped God's holy word would have an influence on the hearts of the employers. The *Derbyshire Courier* said it believed this was the first time in the county that a minister of the Church of England had invited a body of strikers to attend a service in a church.

Strike parade, Stoney Middleton. The banner is believed to be from the Workers Union. They were strong in Sheffield amongst workers in the armaments industry and raised money for the strikers. A women's branch was formed there in 1918. The man in the trilby hat in front of the banner is believed to be Bill ('Willie') Slater, with his wife Ruth. Slater was the NUBSO branch secretary sacked by Ridgeway Brothers.

Although NUBSO had tried to avoid a strike, once called the great majority of workers supported it. Doris Coates described them as 'an unlikely bunch of militants' but they proved themselves to be an extremely loyal and resourceful bunch. A small number of operatives did remain at work, and employers brought in family members to join the 'accommodators'. (The terms 'scab' and 'blackleg' were also used). Gifts and promises of better conditions were offered, whilst hunger and fear were powerful factors.

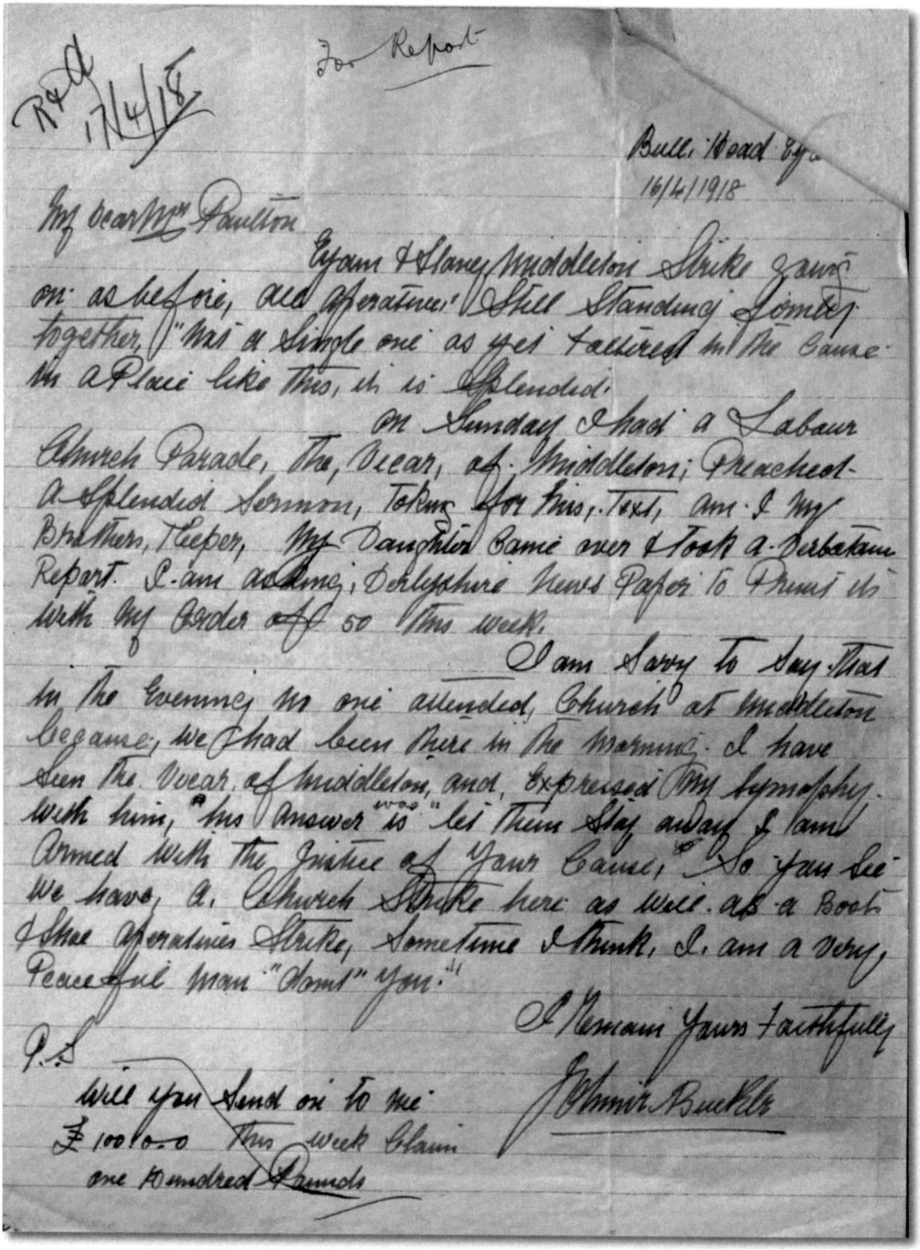

Rec'd 17/4/18

For Report

Bull's Head Eyam
16/4/1918

My dear Mr Poulton

Eyam & Stoney Middleton Strike going on as before, all operatives still standing firmly together, not a single one as yet faltered in the cause in a place like this, it is splendid.

On Sunday I had a Labour Church Parade, the Vicar of Middleton preached a splendid sermon, taking for his text, am I my brother's keeper, my daughter came over & took a verbatim report. I am asking Derbyshire News Paper to print it with my order of 50 this week.

I am sorry to say that in the evening no one attended church at Middleton because we had been there in the morning. I have seen the Vicar of Middleton and expressed my sympathy with him, his answer was "let them stay away I am armed with the justice of your cause," so you see we have a church strike here as well as a Boot & Shoe operatives strike, sometime I think I am a very peaceful man "don't" you."

I remain yours faithfully

Johnnie Buckle

P.S.

Will you send on to me £100.0.0 this week claim one hundred pounds

John Buckle's letter to Edward Poulton, NUBSO General Secretary about the 'splendid' solidarity of the strikers, and the service at St. Martin's Church. Note the vicar's comment that he was 'armed with the justice' of their cause.

An indication of the strike's impact came at a tribunal hearing in Bakewell in June. Ridgeway's were making a case for one of their workers - not a union member - to be exempted from conscription. Their representative said that as a result of the strike and army service, the firm's output was only one quarter of what it would normally be. The firm only had seven men left and claimed that if they lost this individual as well, the business could close. "The strike had affected his trade very much and there was no sign of the men coming back." We know from union reports that 62 workers from Ridgeway Brothers were on strike. So, the employer's claim to the Ministry of Labour and local magistrate, William Nixon that there was no dispute seems to be at odds with what they said at the tribunal.

In June 1918, Member of Parliament and leader of the National Union of General Workers (formerly the gas workers), Will Thorne addressed a crowd in Eyam (pictured above looking south across The Square. The shop on the left is now a private residence). He talked of the risk of industrial war following the World War if British employers didn't change tack. He said, "the soldiers and sailors who fought for their country would expect a greater share of their nation's wealth". The parade to the rally was headed by 'Private H. May, drawn in a bath chair, who had lost his leg on active service. He desired to give his support to the operatives'. (*Derbyshire Courier 29.06.1918*) Thorne asked questions in Parliament about the strike and the refusal of employers to engage in talks. He tried to get the Ministry of Labour to intervene, as NUBSO had done earlier, but was unsuccessful.

Support for the strike was remarkably solid. The NUBSO branch retained a membership of around 160 throughout the first year of the strike. Organiser John Buckle said he "had never had a more loyal or stauncher army of strikers". Local magistrate William Nixon, however, was concerned about damage to the social fabric of the villages arising from the dispute and tried to bring the sides together. His efforts were turned down by the employers.

The strikers achieved a notable victory in May when Heginbotham's signed an agreement with the union. After improving wages for their 1916 war order for Russian boots, it seems that the firm had reverted to lower pay and longer hours. They needed nationally agreed wages and conditions to seek further war contracts. Hours were reduced from 59 to 50 and wages went up 60%, but union hopes that this would influence other firms were dashed when the employers turned down a further arbitration offer.

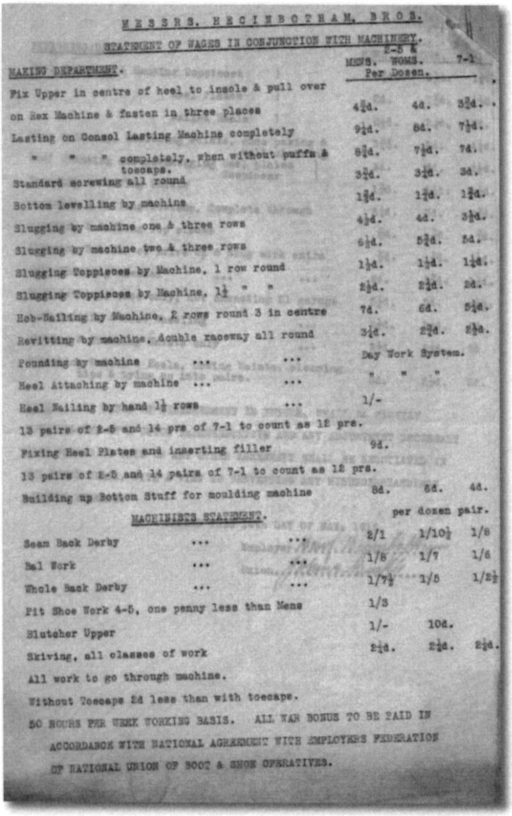

MESSRS. HEGINBOTHAM, BROS.

STATEMENT OF WAGES IN CONJUNCTION WITH MACHINERY.

MAKING DEPARTMENT.	MENS.	2-5 & WOMS.	7-1
	Per Dozen.		
Fix Upper in centre of heel to insole & pull over on Rex Machine & fasten in three places	4¾d.	4d.	3¾d.
Lasting on Consol Lasting Machine completely	9¼d.	8d.	7½d.
" " " completely, when without puffs & toecaps.	8¼d.	7½d.	7d.
Standard screwing all round	3¾d.	3½d.	3d.
Bottom levelling by machine	1¾d.	1½d.	1¼d.
Slugging by machine one & three rows	4½d.	4d.	3½d.
Slugging by machine two & three rows	6½d.	5¾d.	5d.
Slugging Toppieces by Machine, 1 row round	1½d.	1½d.	1¼d.
Slugging Toppieces by Machine, 1½ " "	2½d.	2¼d.	2d.
Hob-Nailing by Machine, 2 rows round 3 in centre	7d.	6d.	5¼d.
Revitting by machine, double raceway all round	3¼d.	2¾d.	2½d.
Pounding by machine	Day Work System.		
Heel Attaching by machine	"	"	"
Heel Nailing by hand 1½ rows ...	1/-		
13 pairs of 2-5 and 14 prs of 7-1 to count as 12 prs.			
Fixing Heel Plates and inserting filler	9d.		
13 pairs of 2-5 and 14 pairs of 7-1 to count as 12 prs.			
Building up Bottom Stuff for moulding machine	8d.	6d.	4d.

MACHINISTS STATEMENT.

	per dozen pair.		
Seam Back Derby	2/1	1/10½	1/8
Bal Work	1/8	1/7	1/6
Whole Back Derby	1/7½	1/5	1/2½
Pit Shoe Work 4-5, one penny less than Mens	1/3		
Blutcher Upper	1/-	10d.	
Skiving, all classes of work	2¼d.	2½d.	2½d.

All work to go through machine.

Without Toecaps 2d less than with toecaps.

50 HOURS PER WEEK WORKING BASIS. ALL WAR BONUS TO BE PAID IN ACCORDANCE WITH NATIONAL AGREEMENT WITH EMPLOYERS FEDERATION OF NATIONAL UNION OF BOOT & SHOE OPERATIVES.

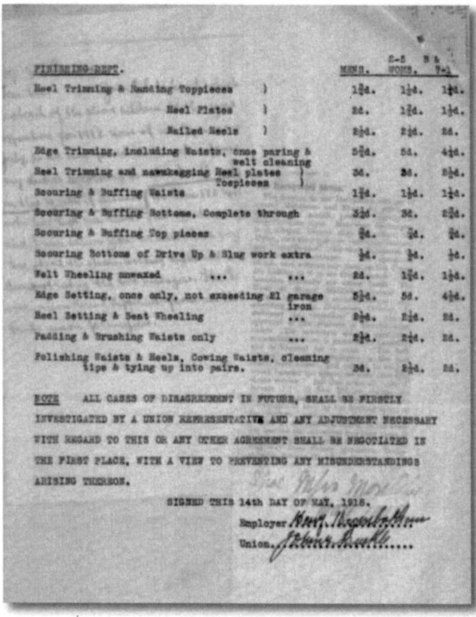

FINISHING DEPT.	MENS.	2-5 & WOMS.	7-1
Heel Trimming & Sanding Toppieces	1¾d.	1½d.	1¼d.
Heel Plates	2d.	1½d.	1½d.
Nailed Heels	2½d.	2¼d.	2d.
Edge Trimming, including Waists, once paring & welt cleaning	5½d.	5d.	4½d.
Heel Trimming and [illegible] Heel plates / Toepieces	3d.	3d.	2½d.
Scouring & Buffing Waists	1¾d.	1½d.	1¼d.
Scouring & Buffing Bottoms, Complete through	3½d.	3d.	2¾d.
Scouring & Buffing Top pieces	¾d.	¾d.	¾d.
Scouring Bottoms of Drive Up & Slug work extra	½d.	½d.	½d.
Welt Wheeling unwaxed	2d.	1¾d.	1½d.
Edge Setting, once only, not exceeding 21 garage iron	5½d.	5d.	4½d.
Heel Setting & Seat Wheeling ...	2½d.	2¼d.	2d.
Padding & Brushing Waists only ...	2½d.	2¼d.	2d.
Polishing Waists & Heels, Cowing Waists, cleaning tips & tying up into pairs.	3d.	2½d.	2d.

NOTE ALL CASES OF DISAGREEMENT IN FUTURE, SHALL BE FIRSTLY INVESTIGATED BY A UNION REPRESENTATIVE AND ANY ADJUSTMENT NECESSARY WITH REGARD TO THIS OR ANY OTHER AGREEMENT SHALL BE NEGOTIATED IN THE FIRST PLACE, WITH A VIEW TO PREVENTING ANY MISUNDERSTANDINGS ARISING THEREON.

SIGNED THIS 14th DAY OF MAY, 1918.

Employer............

Union............

The agreement signed in May 1918 between NUBSO and Heginbotham's. (pictured above and left). Crucially, the firm agreed to union conditions on hours and wages, including a war bonus, and recognised that NUBSO would need to be involved in settling any future disagreements.

The employers' apparent belief that winter would force strikers to seek re-employment proved to be unfounded. The strike moved into its second year with no resolution in sight at the remaining firms.

There is evidence in 1919 that Heginbotham's were finishing work for other firms still involved with the dispute, going against the spirit of the agreement. However, NUBSO decided against a further strike there because of the improvements already achieved.

Defying employer hostility, winter hardship, lack of money and the Spanish flu epidemic, the boot and shoemakers stood together and kept the strike going through 1919, and then into the following year. At least two of the strikers, Kate Hall and Mary Willis died from 'Spanish flu'.

From 1918 to 1920, the Spanish flu pandemic affected large parts of the world. In Britain alone an estimated 228,000 people died and around a quarter of the population was affected. As many as 50 million people worldwide are believed to have perished. Early reports of the pandemic were censored because of concerns about the likely effects on troop morale.

The strikers probably never imagined the dispute would last so long. Unintentionally, they became part of a much wider picture of industrial unrest which swept through the country in 1919 and 1920. The Government was so worried about strikes and mutinies by soldiers and sailors seeking demobilisation, that they sent a battleship down the Mersey and deployed troops in Liverpool, Glasgow, Luton and other British cities and towns.

In Eyam and Stoney Middleton, the immediate issue was helping families keep going. A strong sense of solidarity and mutual support in the community were crucial. Most companies had just enough staff to keep producing, and so felt they could face down the strike. Had the railway workers union responded to NUBSO's appeal, however and stopped transport of supplies and footwear the result may have been very different.

Despite their own hardship, strikers raised money for other causes such as 'The Soldiers and Sailors Comfort Fund' and for local children. Strikers' spirits were raised by the widespread support they received.

Many of the men found other work, for example in local fluorspar mines and gravel pits, which helped to tide them over as families found it hard to manage on strike pay alone. The union also arranged for sewing machines to be placed in some homes, so that women workers could try and earn some money as well. This was part of the preparation for the strikers establishing their own factory. (See next chapter)

NUBSO members from all round the country sent donations. Sheffield munitions workers were especially active at raising money to support the strikers, but the strikers faced real difficulties. Making ends meet included being able to pay the rent. Many homes were owned by the employers or their friends. Strikers faced possible eviction if they failed to maintain rent payments.

Doris Coates recalls her parents being too proud to seek Poor Relief and refusing to run up debt. Her mother "'vainly trudged around the bigger houses trying to get domestic work". The children contributed too, for example by running errands to earn extra coppers (*pennies*). "Each day brought the fear of hunger".

After such a long time on strike, and with no immediate prospect of a breakthrough, the strikers and their union needed fresh ideas. It was John Buckle who came up with a potentially ground-breaking way forward.

Friendly Society membership provided a lifeline in times of sickness and unemployment. The 'Oddfellows' was a working class organisation run by its members. The Independent Order of Oddfellows, Manchester Unity, which included the Eyam and Stoney Middleton Lodges was established in 1810. The society would provide sickness benefit or convalescence after an injury, 8s each week before the war. The annual membership was considered a good insurance at a time when there was no health service, and most workers weren't entitled to unemployment benefit. The Dawson family paid a subscription of 3s 4d a month in 1912.

Club Row in Eyam was originally owned by the Oddfellows until it was eventually sold to the council in the 1970s. Its name came from the nickname of the Society.

Chapter five - Breaking dawn

"The story of the establishment of trades unions (in Eyam and Stoney Middleton) is a remarkable one and the fight for it is the longest in the history of the National Union of Boot and Shoe Operatives. The sequel however is almost as remarkable....and is as much along the lines of the most modern movement as the action of the employers in objecting to a Trades Union was a reversion to old fashioned...prejudices."

Derby Mercury, October 1st, 1920.

The co-operative factory in Eyam *(Derby Mercury 1st October 1920)*

The striking workers had survived the harsh winter of 1918/19 and support remained strong. The union members had confounded the expectations of their employers who thought the strike would crumble in the cold winter months.

Trade unionists from around the country continued to make donations to the strike fund, but the prospects for a settlement still seemed remote. To try and alleviate the desperate situation, NUBSO organiser John Buckle started work on the idea of setting up a new factory to provide employment for the strikers.

Modern day view from Tideswell Lane

It's not clear whether Buckle's initiative was an attempt to force the employers' hand in negotiations, or more of a back-up plan should the strike fail, or perhaps both. The *Derbyshire Courier* of 12th July 1919 saw it as a plan to beat the employers, but there was also a pressing practical need. A new factory could provide work and much needed income and give the strikers a constructive project to work on and hope for a better future.

Whatever the reasons, it was a bold and innovative decision, more so because the workers envisaged running the new factory on co-operative lines. Buckle said that the questions asked by Will Thorne in Parliament the previous year had assisted his efforts to get a certificate to erect a new factory. He believed labour would be purchased at its true value, and older hands could give instruction to younger women workers. Ultimately, he saw the scheme bringing happiness and prosperity to the district.

Finding land for such a venture however was a difficult task. A letter to a local newspaper in March 1919 suggests that employers were trying to block the initiative, saying that no landowner would sell land to the union. Buckle later also complained about a local friendly society (the Penny Thrift Society) which he said had treated the union very badly during attempts to purchase land for the factory.

Eventually the union was able to obtain a plot of land just off Tideswell Lane in Eyam, possibly with the help of one of its own members who had a house and land close by. The workers' union NUBSO loaned Buckle £250 to buy an army hut measuring 80 x 15 foot, and funds also came from outside donations (totaling £160), from NUBSO branches, and the *Daily Herald* newspaper.

In June 1919, John Buckle addressed members and supporters at a rally and said he hoped to have machinery and work for the co-operative factory within a fortnight and they could start training up younger members.

"The dawn was breaking" Buckle told the crowd. "There would be no more tyranny. They were (to be) free men and women, free all the time from the old order of things" (*Derbyshire Courier*, 7th June 1919).

Getting the factory established owed much to Buckle's commitment and hard work - he was doing this work in addition to his full-time job as one of the union's two national organisers. He had support from the Co-operative Wholesale Society (CWS) which helped to erect the army hut and equip it with machinery for closing uppers. Assistance also came from what might seem an unlikely source, Henry Trickett Ltd, a Lancashire footwear manufacturer.

Trickett's was unusual in being a very forward thinking and progressive company, which recognized its employees' trade union, paid for holiday leave, had a 48 hour week (10 hours less than in Eyam and Stoney Middleton), and provided insurance for death benefit, and refreshments and sports facilities for its workers. The company appeared willing to advise the firms involved in the strike, but the local employers weren't prepared to meet Trickett's. John Buckle did meet with Trickett's Managing Director in Manchester, possibly to see how they could support the new co-operative venture. However, it's not clear if this was mainly to glean information and gain advice, or whether it was followed up with practical assistance.

Getting the new factory going was clearly a difficult task, but its success also needed the strikers' willingness to try something new. This they were prepared to do, with women working at home to start with, undergoing training and then moving into the new premises in 1920. Some of the strikers worked as labourers, preparing the site for the hut, making a roadway and helping to put up a small stone building for an engine house.

The hut was erected, and stone building finished by skilled workers brought in and paid out of the funds raised (*see insert of letter listing costs*). About 40 machines were installed, probably obtained from a Co-operative Wholesale Society factory in Leicester, along with a gas engine to drive the machinery. Initially around 40 women were employed, with perhaps up to

60 at one point, with shorter hours, and wages more than double their previous earnings. Willie Slater (the NUBSO branch secretary) was appointed manager of the factory, and an 'expert machinist' from Leicester was brought in to train the operatives on what was described as a new class of work. According to Buckle, they were seeking work of a higher quality than other local factories in order to bring in more money to the village.

A view inside the co-operative factory

The plan was for the buildings and machinery to be owned by the workers, and for all operatives to be shareholders after 18 months.

John Buckle also hoped to set up another factory in the village. This would enable all the strikers to obtain work, and the whole process of making boots and shoes could be done in the village, rather than just closing the uppers. This however proved to be a more ambitious plan than they could manage in the difficult economic circumstances.

Early reports suggested the new factory was very successful. The women have 'set themselves with a will to the tasks. They have proved so efficient that they are able within three months to turn out a larger quantity of work than was at first estimated.' (*Derby Mercury, see article on p. 76*)

COPY.

National Union of Boot and Shoe Operatives.

EYAM BRANCH.

11th March 1923.

Dear Mr.Buckle,

I herewith enclose you the information as required.

Paid to Mr.Poynton, towards Gas Engine.	£ 50.0.0.
Paid for conveying hut from Leicester to Eyam.	£ 10.9.9.
Paid for the slating of Hut.	£ 61.4.6.
Paid for Engine House, including Road to same.	£255.12.3.
Paid for laying of pipes, re Gas Main.	£ 61.19.10
Paid to E.Dane, Joiner, for Wood Closet.	£ 17.10.0.
Paid to Singers Sewing Machine Co.,	£ 4.2.4.
We have also paid in Railway Carr, and to and from Grindleford Station, also in Board and Lodging for men erecting Hut.	£ 90.2.0.
Also Paid to Hathersage Gas Co. for Gas consumed.	£ 64.11.8.
Paid to National Gas Engine Co, for Oil.	£ 13.0.9.
Total.	£. 628.13.1.

(Signed) W.Slater.

Secretary.

List of building costs for the co-operative factory

MERCURY, FRIDAY, OCTOBER 1, 1920.

"DIRECT ACTION" IN NORTH DERBYSHIRE.

A Strike which Lasted Two-and-a-Half Years.

WORKERS START THEIR OWN FACTORY.

("MERCURY" SPECIAL).

The village of Eyam, in the Peak of Derbyshire, is noted for the self-sacrificing labours of its Vicar in the year 1666 in trying to overcome the plague which had attacked his parishioners. Eyam is likely to become famous also, at least in the history of industrial struggles, as surely one of the last places in England where a fight had to be made for the recognition of Trades Unionism.

Further, Eyam will have a claim to fame as a place where the workers, having stood their ground, with true Derbyshire grit, for two and a half years, decided to venture on a bit of "direct action" of a constructive kind.

The story of the establishment of trades unionism in Eyam is a remarkable one, and the fight for it is the longest in the history of the National Union of Boot and Shoe Operatives, which extends to nearly half a century. The sequel, however, is almost as remarkable as the cause of the strike, and is as much along the lines of the most modern movement, as the action of the employers in objecting to a Trades Union was a reversion to old-fashioned early eighteenth century prejudices.

COMING OF THE UNION.

The boot and shoe factories were started in Eyam and its neighbouring village of Stoney Middleton about a dozen years ago. At Eyam there was undertaken ankle and bar-shoe work, and at Stoney Middleton it was mostly pit boots that were made. Altogether, about 500 operatives were employed when the factories got into full swing. The owners, we believe, were men who had themselves been operatives in the first place, but saw their opportunity, seized it, and became employers of their fellow-villagers.

On the first day of the year 1918 there descended on the village one whom the local employers did not regard with a favourable eye at all, although he had generally been able to work amicably with the masters in other parts of the country, and had exercisede a moderating influence at times when disputes in the boot and shoe industry had occurred. This was Mr. J. Buckle, J.P., the Union Organiser, who thought it was time that the operatives in this secluded Peak district should be brought into line with their fellows elsewhere. He gave an address on trade unionism, with the result that it was resolved to form a branch at Eyam and Stoney Middleton. Officers and committee were appointed, and the branch was in being.

But the employers of the district did not see why their employees should not be content to work as they had done in the past without any organisation. They knew what [illegible] These dismissals were followed by the moving of [illegible] other members of the branch committee [illegible] operatives altogether were deprived of their employment at the factories. In all cases the reason given for their dismissal was because they had joined the Union. [illegible]

THE SPIRIT OF THE PEOPLE.

But if the employers had counted upon this harsh action to bring the employees to their knees, and break up the Union at the start, they had very seriously under-estimated the spirit of their people. The latter seem to partake of the nature of the rugged hills which surround their homes, and the wild swelling moorlands which separate them from the rest of their fellows. Silent and strong, they were determined that, having taken a step which they deemed would be to their interest, there should be no turning back. The Union officials endeavoured to bring about a settlement, and, on the advice of the Union Organiser, the remainder of the operatives continued at their work. National officials tried to have an interview with the employers, but the latter refused to see them or to have anything to do with them. They even declined the invitation of Lord Askwith, as Chief Commissioner of the Government Industrial Department, to attend a Conference to talk matters over.

When all attempts at conciliation had failed it was reluctantly decided that drastic action must be taken by the operatives, who thereupon handed in their notices. They demanded recognition of the Union, reduction of the hours of work from 59 to 52½ per week, payment of the National war bonus, and reinstatement of all operatives discharged for joining the Union.

£9,000 IN STRIKE PAY.

For over two and a half years the operatives have remained as obdurate as the masters. For that length of time some thousands of pounds' worth of machinery in the factories has remained silent; only about a dozen machines in a factory or two being kept at work recently by a few people who, of course, are not members of the Union.

For about two and a half years the Union has stood at the back of the operatives, and regularly dispensed strike pay. This has amounted to the total of over £9,000. At the same time, as there seems to be no prospect of the masters yielding, Mr. Buckle, the Union Organiser, who took a special personal interest in the village, promised some machines, and installed these in the homes of some of the people, and gave them work, which he was able to obtain from various outside employers. Many of the men obtained other work in the district, such as quarrying or helping on the farms.

As time went on, and the employers resisted all attempts at intervention, not only on the part of Government Departments, but of local gentlemen, and, in particular, Mr. J. Nixon, the chief magistrate of the district, Mr. Buckle recognised that some con[illegible] He therefore decided that a factory should be started and run by the workers.

A BOLD PROJECT.

This was a bold idea, especially as there was no capital available, and the workers, after depending on strike pay for over two years had no money to put into such a venture. Difficulties of this kind, however, did not daunt Mr. Buckle. He appealed to a number of friends, and through them secured sufficient money to purchase a military hut, 80ft. by 15ft., for which he had to give £250. A plot of land was obtained at a yearly rental of a small sum, on the outskirts of the village, and there some of the strikers worked as manual labourers, preparing the site for the hut, and making a roadway, and helping to put up a small stone building.

The skilled workers employed on building had to be employed week by week, and the money had to be found. Difficulties, however, exist to be overcome, and gradually the work progressed until the engine-house, built of stone, obtained from a site at the other end of the village bought by the organiser, was finished, and the hut was placed in position, opening into the stone structure. A gas engine was fixed in the building, shafting was run down the whole length of the hut, and forty to fifty machines of various kinds required in a boot factory, were put in, all worked by the gas engine.

This work was completed rather more than two months ago, and as soon as ready forty women and girls who had been on strike started work. They had previously been used to a rather simple kind of work, making ankle and bar-shoe uppers, but it was determined that a better and more complete class of work should be done.

They are now making practically the whole of the uppers for children's boots and shoes, and for this work many of the women had to learn how to work different machines from those to which they had been used in order to carry out the many and varied processes. They have set themselves with a will to these tasks, and under the tuition of Mr. Buckle and Mr. Slater, the manager, they have proved so efficient that they are able within three months to turn out a larger quantity of work than was at first estimated when taking contracts from firms.

BETTER CONDITIONS AND PAY.

Under the old conditions the women's wages did not average 13s. a week, and most of them, we understand, did not receive much more than 10s. For two months in the new factory, under the trade union rules, they have been paid at least £2 a week, and now, having learnt how to work the machines, they are being paid by results. The consequence is that most of them, if not all, are earning nearer £2 10s. a week than £2, and when in full swing will no doubt obtain £3. Instead of working 59 hours they are employed only 43 to 48 a week.

The cost of the work so far is about £2,000, but there is need of working capital, and the aim is to get this in hand. Already there is a project afoot for extensions, and on the piece of ground at the other end of the village [illegible] erected as soon as possible a [illegible] where the men may be employed. The intention is to make the whole of the boot or shoe, instead of uppers only, as at present.

There are great possibilities in this experiment, and under such conditions as now prevail there can be little doubt that this venture on the part of the workers, who can carry on a more extensive work than before, will lead to far better results for themselves and increased happiness. With careful management it may develop into a factory on a big scale, employing practically all the available male and female labour of the district.

BELPER WAR MEMORIAL. | MATLOCK BATH FESTIVAL. | MELBOURNE PETTY SESSIONS.

Article in the *Derby Mercury* about the strike and new factory.

The new venture (known variously as the 'Ideal Closing' or 'Ideal Shoe' factory) was seen as a beacon of hope. Even during its short life, the workers showed how workplaces could be run in a different way, and that an alternative model of production was possible.

'The village of Eyam is noted for the self-sacrificing labours of its vicar... in 1666 in trying to overcome the plague... Eyam is likely to become famous also as surely one of the last places where a fight had to be made for the recognition of trade unionism.

Further, Eyam will have a claim to fame as a place where the workers, having stood their ground with true Derbyshire grit for two and a half years decided... on direct action of a constructive kind.'

(Derby Mercury)

The early success of the new factory, employing most of the women still on strike, and the fact that many of the men had found other work, led NUBSO to end the strike in 1920. The union had spent £8445 on strike pay. (NUBSO National Council Report, 23rd August 1920)

Unfortunately, over the next two years, the 'Ideal Closing' factory ran into difficulties. There was a recession in the industry throughout the country in 1920/1921 and the main firm providing orders ended its contract. The other local footwear firms were, according to local accounts hostile to the new venture, seeing it as a threat to their businesses. With little income and capital, the factory struggled to remain viable, a common problem elsewhere at that time for co-operative enterprises. Despite his best efforts, John Buckle could not obtain further orders, and the decision was reluctantly made in 1922 to close the factory. The financial affairs of the company were wound up in 1923, and the CWS was approached for help in paying back loans and defraying the personal debts Buckle had accrued in setting the factory up.

The first phase of a long struggle which had started 5 years earlier was over. The union had failed to get recognition or win its other demands in most of the firms (Heginbotham's being the exception) but the strikers had still achieved a great deal. They left a legacy which would be picked up by others, and sowed seeds which would bear fruit in later years.

Chapter six - The legacy, sowing the seeds

The strike lasted nearly two and a half years. The co-operative factory then operated for two years. Many of the families involved faced great difficulties when the strike ended, and others struggled after the new factory was forced into closure and the women there lost their jobs. The union continued to support those who could not get a job or who were sick, by paying out benefits.

It is thought that several individual workers and families had to leave the two villages to look for work elsewhere, some because of 'blacklisting' by the employers. There was a shortage of other jobs locally in 1921 as the economy went into recession. Harry Dawson, for example had to seek work in a Sheffield foundry, and was only able to return home to see his family on Saturdays and stay for one night because of his long shifts.

We know that the population of Eyam declined around that time, but we can't be sure whether families moved away because of their involvement with the strike, the legacy of the war or because of a general shortage of work in the area.

The strike started at the same time as news was still reaching homes of the losses of young men fighting in the war. When hostilities ended, workers were still on strike. It took many months before some of the local men and women in uniform were able to return to civilian life. Those who had previously worked in the boot and shoe trade had to decide whether to support the strike or be used as strike breakers. There were former soldiers on both sides.

Local magistrate, William Nixon, who'd tried to bring both sides together, was very concerned that the dispute would cause social tensions in the villages in the years ahead. His prediction is hard to prove, but it is likely that the tensions remained for quite a while after the strike finished. It appears that many participants simply didn't talk much about the events, and this may have been a way of trying to avoid conflict with neighbours or fellow workers, and of protecting their children from being caught up in it. The fact that some of the strikers were eventually taken back by their old employers could also help to explain why people didn't talk much about the strike.

For those who were working in the shoe factories after the strike, their employers were in a stronger position having successfully resisted the union's demands. Heginbotham's may have been the only firm to accept the union, but other factory owners went back on their earlier vows not to employ strikers. They needed to take back some of the union members in order to have enough staff to remain viable. NUBSO believed, with some justification, that the strike had brought benefit to the local boot and shoe trade, and other industries in the area. (*National Council* report, 23rd Aug. 1920)

The establishment of the new co-operative factory in Eyam, paying higher wages and offering shorter hours, probably played a key part in improving employment conditions in all the factories as employers vied to retain and attract staff. This was especially significant for the women, who for the first time got paid a proper union rate. Elsewhere in the industry the first calls for equal pay were also emerging. The settlement at Heginbotham's had shown that it was possible for the union to gain a foothold in the factories, and that wages and conditions could be significantly improved despite employer opposition to trade unions. A precedent had been set.

Other workers in the area were also inspired by the boot and shoemakers to join unions. The National Union of General Workers (NUGW), for example, organised workers in a diverse range of local industries, including limestone quarries in Matlock, Buxton and Wirksworth, the Derwent Valley Water Board, spar mines near Eyam, the Edale cotton mill, Eastwood Chemicals in Castleton, and lead mines in Bradwell. They secured good wage increases for many workers, and established union branches in Bradwell and Eyam with a total of around 800 members in the area. The NUGW branch in Eyam had been set up with the help of John Buckle and Bill Slater. The financial support for the strike from workers in Sheffield and from the NUGW at a national level illustrated the close connections between the two unions. Will Thorne's visits to Eyam were evidence of solidarity, and also gratitude for the assistance given by the Eyam NUBSO branch to his union and its local members.

Over the years, and especially after the start of the Second World War, with the rise in demand for army boots, the factory owners realised that they were better served co-operating with the unions. In 1941, a local NUBSO branch was restarted in Stoney Middleton, and the remaining four larger firms recognised the National Union of Boot and Shoe Operatives and accepted national wages and conditions.

The four local firms were Ridgeway and Willis (formerly Ridgeway and Fox), West and Sons (both in Eyam), Wm. Lennon's (in Stoney Middleton) and Heginbotham Brothers (now in Calver). So the seeds sown over 20 years earlier had at last borne fruit. NUBSO recruited nearly all the workers in these four firms and maintained its organisation and representation after the war ended.

NUBSO merged with three other unions in 1971 to form the National Union of Footwear, Leather and Allied Trades (NUFLAT). Twenty years later, as the decline of traditional industries led to job losses, the enlarged union again merged, this time with the hosiery and knitwear workers to create the National Union of Knitwear, Footwear and Apparel Trades (KFAT). In 2004 a further series of mergers began leading to the development of the 'Community' union. Organising workers in a diverse range of sectors, from steel to boot making and community care, the new organisation took a different approach to many other unions by trying to organise in and with communities badly affected by de-industrialisation. At the time of writing, Community is still the union representing workers in boot and shoemaking, including those at Lennon's in Stoney Middleton, the last local firm left from the time of the strike.

PARLIAMENTARY ELECTION
DECEMBER, 1910.
Western Division of Derbyshire.
CHAS. F. WHITE
THE LIBERAL AND PEOPLE'S CANDIDATE,
respectfully solicits your
VOTE AND INTEREST.

'Visions of a Fairer Life'

The plight of the shoemakers, war widows and others at the 'sharp end' of life, was to receive a powerful voice in Parliament when Charles Frederick White, himself a shoemaker and repairer, and self-declared 'people's candidate', was elected as the Member of Parliament for West Derbyshire in the 'khaki election' of 1918. White stood as an independent Liberal, refusing to go along with his Party's alliance (under Lloyd George) with the Conservative and Unionist Party.

Charles White (left) election leaflet, 1910.

He didn't get elected in 1910 but in the 1918 general election he achieved a famous victory.

There were sharp divisions in the villages over the rival candidates. Footwear employers like Isaac Ridgeway supported the Conservative and Unionist, Lord Kerry, who was a brother in law of the Duke of Devonshire. Many of the strikers, on the other hand were active in White's campaign, and Laurel Cottage, the Dawson family home in Eyam, became a hub of local activity for his supporters. The Labour Party didn't stand a candidate.

White's famous victory over Kerry was the first time a candidate linked to the Devonshire/Cavendish family had ever been defeated in the constituency. Doris Coates was probably speaking on behalf of many involved in White's campaign when she later said of the election that 'working people had challenged the rich and powerful and triumphed.'

Following the success of the suffrage movement at the time, millions of women over 30 were able to vote for the first time in a general election. White supported women's suffrage and believed women's support for him was a crucial factor in his success. He was an active and committed local MP, and managed to hold the seat in the 1922 election. Sadly, for his family and supporters, however White became ill and died the following year at the age of 60.

The seat returned to the Conservative dominance of the aristocratic Cavendish family. However, some years later in 1944 another extraordinary political upset saw Charles White's son of the same name, win a majority in a by-election, taking the seat from the Conservative Party. Standing as an Independent Labour candidate, Charlie White defeated William Cavendish (The Marquis of Hartington), son of the Duke of Devonshire. It is quite likely that some of the strikers and their families from 1918 would have campaigned and voted for White as they had done for his father before.

Hannah Mitchell (left), born in the Peak District, became an active and prominent campaigner for women's suffrage in the Manchester area.

John Buckle, The NUBSO organiser who had done so much to support boot and shoemakers in Eyam and Stoney Middleton, later also became an MP. He was elected to the House of Commons in 1922 for the Eccles constituency in Lancashire, unseating the Conservative incumbent. He held the seat the year after, but lost it following the fall of the minority Labour Government in 1924. He died in 1925, aged just 58. He had created a close bond of friendship with many people in the two villages and was held in high regard by the boot and shoemakers who joined the union.

Doris Coates, daughter of shoemaker and striker Harry Dawson, believed the events of the day showed the possibility of 'improving life by our own efforts'. She saw education as a crucial avenue for advancement, especially for girls. Despite her own limited elementary schooling, she managed to gain entry to Goldsmith's College in London where she trained as a teacher. She was the first student to be accepted at Goldsmith's who had not been to grammar school. Others followed Doris's example.

A campaign developed in the area to establish a secondary school. After many years of lobbying, the opening up of access to education after the Second World War and with Charlie White leading Derbyshire County Council, the campaigners achieved success. Hope Valley College, in the village of Hope, opened its doors in September 1958. All children from Eyam and other villages in the area would now have the chance to go to secondary school.

It is clear when talking to residents of the two villages that a great resilience and community spirit had developed and been sustained despite the deaths in the two great wars and the decline of some local industries like footwear. As transport links improved between the villages and the urban areas of Sheffield, Chesterfield and Derby, it became easier for the surviving industry to attract new markets, and for visitors to come to the newly formed Peak District National Park, created in 1951. Charlie White MP, son of the Charles White elected back in 1918, was chairman of the new Peak Park Planning Board.

Eyam became a focus for the fast-developing tourist industry as people flocked to see for themselves the legacy of the plague of 1665-66, as well as the Peak District traditions of Well Dressings and carnivals. Today thousands of people visit the two villages to join celebrations of modern village life whilst looking back on historical events. Eyam Museum plays a key role in helping visitors, especially school children, make sense of the past in order to better understand the present. The Stoney Middleton Heritage Group has played an important part in bringing the history of the village to a wider audience, through interpretation boards, film, discovery trails, publications and its website.

The 'visions of a fairer life' described by Doris Coates were important in helping sustain people and give hope in times of hardship like the war years and the 1930s. But the struggle for union recognition, better working conditions, and improved housing and educational opportunities which her parents' generation fought for is still relevant today. This is the message we received from the Community trade union for our commemorative event in April 2018:

Community trade union sends a message of solidarity to everyone at the centenary strike commemoration in Eyam and Stoney Middleton. Our union organises workers in the footwear industry to this day, carrying on the work of the National Union of Boot and Shoe Operatives, featured in your event.

We pay tribute to the strikers and their families for their courage and determination to achieve the basic right to belong to a union. The two-year strike and the workers' co-operative factory provide an inspiration for all of us today defending the rights of working people. The need for unions is greater than ever considering things like zero hours contracts, the increasing use of food banks for people to feed their families and a national minimum wage that doesn't allow workers access to a decent standard of living.

We stand with you in recognizing all those who paved the way.

Gavin Miller
Midlands Regional Secretary, Community

Wm. Lennon and Co. boot factory in Stoney Middleton is the only one of the original 8 firms involved in the dispute still in business. But along with a new firm in Brough, The Cordwainer, it is maintaining and developing the tradition of boot and shoemaking in the Hope Valley. (See chapter 9)

THE FRESH AIR OF FREEDOM

"It was the lives of our people and their bread and butter we were thinking of. We were struggling to lift ourselves out of....poverty into the fresh air of freedom."

(Will Thorne, reflecting on the purpose of the 'New Unionism' he and others started in the late 19th century. The new general unions were aimed at all workers, whatever their occupation or industry.)

DORIS COATES 'TUNES ON A PENNY WHISTLE'

"My parents...and their friends...taught me how to survive through self-help, and to fight injustice as they had done by their involvement in industrial action and political struggles and countless everyday difficulties. Above all their sense of humour and capacity for fun had prevented me from becoming too solemn."

Chapter seven - Life in the factories, part two

We are lucky to have access to stories of people who worked in or had family connections with the shoe factories through an oral history project in Eyam which started in the 1990s. (Available via the Eyam Museum web site) By threading these conversations together we can begin to get a feel for life in the shoe factories after the First World War and the strike.

"My husband's father owned what was the 'bottom' shoe factory opposite the church, or the rectory gates. My father's grandfather was there too, it's called Leedums now. There were four brothers, and four factories they owned. There was one where Taff's taxis used to be and another at the top of the village; they were all making ladies shoes and slippers. Heginbotham's made the men's shoes and they had a factory at Calver and one in Stoney Middleton".

(Note: The firms Eugenia refers to are probably Ridgeway Brothers – 'the bottom factory'; West's, and Ridgeway & Fox – 'the top factory', which later became Ridgeway and Willis)

Eugenia Ridgeway

"The work wasn't hard, but it was monotonous and boring. In between running errands, I was doing what we call 'solutioning' (gluing). The uppers of the shoes were made of soft leather, before they could put the lining to the upper and turned over so that they could have a neat edge, the edge of the leather were skived away, then it was solutioned, let to dry, turned over and hammered and that made a neat and strong edge.

I think skiving was the word used in all the industry, not just a local word for the process (skiving is the process of thinning the edges of the leather). Later in life when I worked at Dale House, someone I got to know there told me someone she met was a skiver, she said in her defence she wasn't a skiver, that was the other meaning of the word wasn't it?"

Madelaine Cocker

"It were noisy, and dirty, you used to have to brush up every now and then, and one man who were called a clicker, he used to cut all the tops of the leather out, he used to spit, it were awful and then you had to go and sweep up".

Lily Nettleship

Inside West's factory, after the company moved into the former Ridgeway Brothers building at Stanley Works, which later became Leedums.

"I left school at 14 and I went into the shoe factory, West's, (the) one where the taxi man is now. I was expected to go in, I actually wanted to go in there, and I went to become a machinist. We had to make the uppers, they were all in pieces when we got them and we had to put them all together to make what we called a top".

Mary O'Connell

"The women on piece work got no money if there was no sewing work to do, but I still got a wage, 7/6d each week for five and a half days. My wage was really important to me, my mother and father and all worked in the factory, and when he was old enough my younger brother too.

I was working in the shoe factory until I was around 20, nearly six years. It was noisy, not particularly dirty, the machines were noisy, but we were happy. I always found our bosses alright, there were two distinct families had the shoe factories. We worked in the West's factory; the other two factories were owned by the Ridgeways."

Madelaine Cocker

"I left school at 14 on the Friday and we had to go and start work at the factory on the Monday. You'd no choice, because if your father or any of your sisters or brothers worked at the factory, you had to go. Either that or they'd probably sack them, because there were no unions." (Note: Clarice

White started work in Eyam in 1927. She worked a 53-hour week for 8s 0d, around 40p).

Clarice White

"When I left school, I went to work at the shoe factory opposite the church. I learned to be a sewing machinist sewing the uppers of the shoes. By the time you could sew the whole of the upper you began to get on piece work. You got given them in dozens and you got paid so much each dozen. We got 1s 10 1/2d for a dozen pairs, we may get through six dozen pairs in a day. There were thirty odd machinists in there and least twenty blokes. There were only two factories in the village then, around 1947."

Barbara Ashton

"I was happier working in the shoe factory; there were girls my own age. We started work at seven and came out again at eight-thirty for a half hour break for breakfast. We had quite a long walk back up the village. We then worked from nine until one and then two until six, so it was virtually an eleven-hour day with an hour and a half break.

The women who were sewing the tops together, they were on piece work so when there was little work going through they got very little money at all. So when things were slack, the overseer would send me down to where the men were cutting out the pieces of leather all shapes and sizes, she would keep sending me down and sending me down until one day until they got fed up with seeing me, they threw all the lot at me and just threw them at me, I've never forgotten".

Madelaine Cocker

"I have seen the sales book; somebody give me it as rubbish. Before the last war, about 1936 they was selling to the West Indies and all over, they were employing around one hundred and twenty people in the one factory. There was another factory just above the old Rose and Crown pub, that was West's, and Ridgeway and Willis at the top factory". (Note: The sales book referred to was probably for Ridgeway Brothers)

Derek and Paulette Knowles

"It had to close as it was running at a loss, he had to sell it. I never really knew why until I was sat in church one day and this chappie came in wondering what was happening at the shoe factory. He said he had worked there and the owner was a great chap. I told him that was my father in law, he said Tom Ridgeway? and I said yes. He said he was a wonderful man. I told him we never really found out why it closed, and he told me they had been looking for new orders. They got this huge order from one of the mail order catalogue firms, and everyone was delighted because they got this terrific order. They then wanted more and more and then they let, foolishly their other customers down, and the mail order firm started to grind down the price and eventually they were left with $1^{1/2}$d profit for a pair of shoes. You just cannot run a factory and machinery on just that, and he'd lost all his other customers".

Eugenia Ridgeway

Interviews by George May

The full interviews cover many different aspects of village life but show the significance of boot and shoemaking in the lives of many local families. The picture from the interwar period suggests a lot of insecurity with the 1930s depression causing fluctuations in the fortunes of local companies.

Employees couldn't always count on a full working week. Conditions and wages had improved but remained below nationally agreed standards.

Employees worked long hours and men were still expected to bring their daughters to work. During and after the Second World War, conditions and wages improved, and the women interviewed recall being happy at work though the days were still long. Whilst this was partly a reflection of wider changes in society, the re-establishment of trade unions in the factories clearly made a difference, bringing the local firms more in line with other footwear manufacturing districts.

Chapter eight - Centenary year events

Philip Taylor presented an outline history of the local boot and shoe trade to the Eyam Village Society in March 2014. The illustrated talk resulted in much interest in the two villages which led to a series of meetings with members of Stoney Middleton Heritage Group, Eyam Museum committee and local residents. The plan was to start bringing people together to organise commemorative events for 2018, the centenary of the strike.

Following interviews with local people, press releases, local radio interviews and further research, much more information came to light. This led us to the idea of developing a lasting community project including a book at a later date.

The first commemorative event was held at the Wesleyan Reform Chapel in Stoney Middleton in October 2017. The idea was to run a 'History Workshop', to share what information we had already gathered, to display photographs and maps to show where the factories and other places related to the story were located. We asked people to bring along any information they had, and to see if they recognised any of the names of people involved in the local union in 1918-20, in case modern family connections could be made. This would really help to bring the story to life.

Around 80 people came along, far more than anticipated. In fact, it was difficult for everyone to get into the hall and unfortunately some people turned back. Phil presented some slides and talked about the progress we had made collecting information. And then there was a chance to look at the resources and talk about them. We were delighted that so many people came and encouraged by the fact that some of them offered to become involved in a larger planning group which met a few weeks later.

The inaugural meeting of the planning group took place on 13th November 2017 at Stoney Middleton primary school. Invitations were sent to individuals who'd expressed an interest at the History Workshop, and to local organisations such as the Stoney Middleton Heritage Group (who supported the project with part of their Heritage Lottery fund grant), SMILE (a group trying to improve facilities in their village), the well dressers, the two Primary schools, local churches and chapels, parish councils and Eyam Museum.

During November 2017 both Steve and Philip visited Eyam School to work on projects with the schoolchildren. The children covered the shoe history topic as part of their understanding of life in Eyam and its local crafts and industries. This included a visit to Wm Lennon's boot factory and an exciting chance to see first-hand how boots and shoes were made in the past.

Local villagers 'marching with the union' –Stoney Middleton, April 2018.

School children walked from Eyam to Stoney Middleton
(photographs courtesy of Peter Nutkins)

The main event was held on April 14th, 2018. The date was chosen to mark the 100th anniversary of the 'labour church parade' and service organised by the Reverend John Riddlesden and John Buckle from NUBSO (see Chapter 4). Around 250 people including many school children participated in a re-enactment of the 1918 parade. The day's celebrations started in Eyam where the Castleton Silver Band played a selection of tunes. Local residents turned actors for the day, performed a topical play based on the strike story a century earlier. They dressed in the style of the period which gave the whole event a real feel of the times.

More people join the march as it arrives in Stoney Middleton
(photograph courtesy of Peter Nutkins)

Following the music and drama, the participants walked from Eyam to Stoney Middleton taking a route down Lydgate and Mill Lane before being rejoined by the Silver Band near The Bank in Stoney Middleton. Local school children carried banners they had made themselves, and marchers walked and sang along to tunes such as "Marching Through Georgia", with new words which had been specially sung by the legendary jazz musician Acker Bilk. Here is his song 'Marching Union'.

Back in 1873 - twenty-five young men
Organised and organised, and organised again
Now we're 80,000 strong, a power in the land
Marching along with the union.

Chorus: Hurrah! Hurrah! the Union makes us strong
Hurrah! Hurrah! it helps us get along
For shorter hours and higher pay, lets sing our working song
Marching along with the Union

Leather soles or rubber boots and shoes and things
Make 'em for shop stewards, presidents and kings
But when it comes to wages and holidays with pay
We're marching along with the union

Pulling over uppers, finishing the shoe
Singing for your supper ain't quite the thing to do
But we don't mind a song or two to help us celebrate
Marching along with the Union.

The march also featured trade union banners like the parade in support of the shoemakers one hundred years earlier. At the gates of St Martin's Church, a further performance of the 're-enactment' drama captured the conflicting emotions of the dispute, as well as the hard lives endured by so many people at that time.

A service was then held to mark the church's support for the families, in particular the support of the Rev John Riddlesden who preached on the subject of "Am I my brother's keeper?" The service was led by Philip Taylor along with Rev. James Croft and included a reading by Richard Coates, grandson of Harry Dawson who was a prominent figure in the community at the time of the strike. The band played in the church.

Among the hymns sung were 'One more step along the road I go', 'What a friend we have in Jesus' and 'Give me oil in my lamp', interspersed with a dramatic presentation by children from Eyam school, based on a poem "The redundant factory", adapted by Philip from the writing of R. Herbert. Libs Slattery read out letters written by her great grandfather and factory owner, William Lennon, one of whose sons was killed in the First World War. A teacher from Stoney Middleton Primary School read from Doris Coates's book 'Tunes on a Penny Whistle' which recalls her childhood in Eyam at the time of the war and the strike.

Richard Coates reads from
Tunes on a Penny Whistle (left)

Christine Cartledge, from the Wesleyan Reform Chapel read from the memoirs of her grandfather, Tom - a shoemaker from the age of 12, and union member who took part in the strike. Councillor Catherine Tite of the UNITE union made links between the 1918 strike and the important role of unions today. Prayers for peace and reconciliation were said by the Rev. Mike Gilbert from Eyam, who then led The Lord's Prayer. The sharing of the peace preceded the last hymn "I, the Lord of sea and sky" before the final blessing by both local clergy.

After the service guests were able to enjoy refreshments provided by the local Parent Teacher Associations as well as a mobile exhibition about the strike, and a film about the history of Stoney Middleton. (The portable exhibition is available for use in schools and village events. A more permanent display in Eyam Museum opened in May 2018).

The whole commemorative event was filmed by Jack Bowring (on video) with the help of funding from the Heritage Lottery Fund, leaving a lasting documentary record of the day. Professional photographer, Peter Nutkins, also took still photographs of the parade and service.

Three weeks later on bank holiday Monday, the mobile exhibition was on show in Chesterfield Market Hall during the town's May Day Rally, organised by Chesterfield Trades Union Council.

An evening of entertainment took place in the Mechanics Institute in Eyam, designed to replicate the social evenings of 100 years earlier which supported the striking families and also raised money for gifts to send to local men who'd joined the forces. These events were run by local singers and musicians. The hall was lined by photographs and displays from the exhibition and the room soon became very full as the event got under way. The highlight of the evening was an appearance by the popular singer, Bella Hardy from Edale, with other guests including local singer, Andy Hoult, musicians and singers from the Eyam 'Pop Up' Choir; as well as Philip Taylor and his daughter Samantha who performed together as Mason's Apron.

Mason's Apron started proceedings with songs including "Paddy works on the railway" to celebrate the importance of the railways to the local industrial heritage, and "Peg and Awl" about the introduction of machinery into the industry. This was followed by Eyam school children who played a collection of tunes before the 'Pop-Up' Choir took the stage with the songs "Bread and Roses" and "Marching along to the Union".

Bella Hardy took us to the break with songs and tunes on her violin, showing why she has become such a respected performer throughout the UK. A highlight was her first public performance of 'She Lit the Fire' - a superb song written by Simon Haines about the Norfolk schoolteacher, Kitty Higdon and her husband Tom, who were dismissed in 1914 for being too radical in the eyes of the local rector and education authorities. The school children came out on strike in support of their teachers and a strike school was set up which ran for 25 years!

Steve Bond and Jude Hirst read from contemporary accounts of village life and working conditions 100 years ago, giving an insight into the reasons for the strike, the impact of war and the emergence of the women's suffrage movement. They showed how such past times as making music and walking in the nearby countryside provided joy and interest for families in those difficult times.

Mason's Apron started the second half with more working songs "Poverty Knock", The Working Man" and "Part of the Union" before Philip read the poem "The redundant factory floor". He was followed by Andy Hoult with performances of the songs "Union Maid" and "Turning back the clock".

The evening ended with a selection of tunes from the local ukulele band, and a reading of the WW1 poem "In Flanders fields" before Mason's Apron led the rest of the singers and musicians with "Only Remembered", "All the good times are past and gone" and "Rolling Home". An excellent evening was thoroughly enjoyed by all. Proceeds from the event and the April church service went to The Helen's Trust, Bakewell & Eyam Community Transport and the Eyam and Stoney Middleton School PTAs.

The permanent exhibition about the strike, 'The Air of Freedom' opened in Eyam Museum, next to the highly acclaimed World War One display.

The mobile display was again on view at Eyam school's summer fair in July, a regular event organised by the Parent Teacher Association. Richard Coates did several local radio interviews to tell listeners about his mother Doris's book 'Tunes on a Penny Whistle' which had been republished. July's events concluded at Stoney Middleton, where the village Well Dressing group had adopted the shoemakers' strike as the theme for one of their 2018 wells (photograph below) which was designed by Kate Upcraft.

The Well Dressing week was launched by Richard Coates who also wrote the introduction to the programme booklet. The mobile strike exhibition was displayed in the church yard throughout the week.

In October, Philip presented a talk on his work as a shoemaker to Abney Women's Institute, including several slides about the shoemakers' strike, and in November around 500 people attended the various war related exhibits at Hathersage's 100th anniversary Armistice event which included the mobile strike exhibition. Steve also gave talks about the strike to the local Labour Party branch, and to members of Bradwell Historical Society.

Throughout 2018 the strike and the various commemorative events were mentioned in local papers and on the radio, following press releases. We are grateful to all those media organisations for their help in bringing the story to a wider audience.

A local writer, Leslie Oldfield, has written a script for a play about the strike. It is hoped that public performances of the play might be arranged to mark the centenary of the end of the strike.

The mobile exhibition and Tideswell Brass Band at the Stoney Middleton well dressing in 2018

Chapter nine - Today's shoemakers

William Lennon and Co.

William Lennon and his family around the time of World War One.

Better known throughout the boot and shoe industry under the present-day brand of Ruff-lander, William Lennon and Co. continue to make boots using similar techniques and machinery that existed in the hey-day of the industry one hundred years ago.

Founded in 1899, the company has been located at its present site on The Bank since 1903, and it's clear when you enter the door to the factory that you are entering a unique workshop and can sense the history of the company. Now into the fourth generation of the Lennon family, the business is a market leader in the supply of work boots and still exports much of its production. Indeed, it is the only manufacturer of heavy-duty safety boots in Britain. They export boots all over the world as well as acting as agents for a number of brands of world leading industrial and walking boots and shoes.

The factory as seen today.

Les Lennon (pictured left) is William Lennon's grandson. Les managed the company for many years and is a fount of knowledge about the footwear trade and its local history.

Under the present-day stewardship of Libs Slattery (great granddaughter of William Lennon) and her Cousin, Dan, the business continues to thrive in a competitive market. They have kept up their production of good value work boots but have also picked up on a growing market for 'retro' and 'heritage' footwear and can customise their boots and shoes to meet individual tastes as a result of opportunities arising from the internet.

The company has kept up with the times whilst still exuding tradition in the way they manufacture their footwear and maintain traditional skills and expertise in all they do.

Lasts like these with steel sole plates would have been typical of those used by Mason Brothers and Lennon, as well as Heginbotham's in making and repairing boots for the war.

The boot (left) is a replica of the B5 World War One boot made under war office contract. This style is still available from William Lennon and Co. to this date.

Pat Helliwell worked at Wm. Lennon and Co. for 50 years, and was also the union rep. Here she is working on an old 'post' sewing machine.

Post sewing machines were used to sew around the tops of the boot uppers where the work could not be held flat.

William Lennon & Co.
The Bank, Stoney Middleton
Derbyshire. S32 4TD

Telephone: 01433 630451
Website: www.rufflander.co.uk

The Cordwainer.

Although not strictly in the area concerned with the strike, shoemaker Philip Taylor's links with the village of Eyam are sufficient to enable us to list The Cordwainer as among local businesses operating one hundred years after the strike. However, unlike William Lennon and Co., The Cordwainer has only been 'local' since 2010 after relocating from Lancashire.

Philip had already been learning to make shoes when he first came to Eyam aged 19 to visit his grandmother Rose McGuinness, at Upper Burch Row. He considered himself too inexperienced to consider taking on the shoe repair shop in Eyam when he learned it was due to close and preferred to carry on specialising in making orthopaedic footwear instead. Eventually Philip set up his new business in 1996 in Lancashire where he began to build a reputation for the quality of his work helping people with complex mobility problems receive the footwear needed.

Philip moved the business to its present site at Brough near Bradwell in a move partially funded by a grant through the Leader project, European Union support for small businesses to relocate and invest in their new location. Since then the business has become a centre of excellence within the industry, taking on apprentices to build for the future and provide work experience for students from across Europe. Philip's customers come from far and wide, with many spending time in the Peak District to enjoy the scenery and the history of the area.

The Cordwainer's clients come from across the UK and as far away as the United States and Europe as there are so few shoemakers with the skill and experience required solving their footwear problems. His unique insight into the needs and aspirations of people with disabilities comes as a result of having to live with the effects of polio contracted at the age of two. He must wear the footwear his company makes in order to keep him on his feet day to day.

Today's team of young shoemakers should ensure the business continues to develop and grow with the help of new technology alongside the traditional skills required to make bespoke footwear.

The Cordwainer
Unit 8 Brough Business Centre, Bradwell
Derbyshire. S33 9HG

Telephone: 01433 621623
Website: www.thecordwainer.co.uk

Chapter Ten - Union membership, 'not just numbers'

Since 2004, boot and shoe workers throughout the country have been represented by the Community union, following a series of mergers involving NUBSO and other related unions.

We have tried to trace the names of all the boot and shoemakers in Eyam and Stoney Middleton who joined the union and took part in the strike. Fortunately, records do survive of union membership at the time. However, the lists don't give full first names, only initials.

By linking the surnames with census records and other local historical documents, such as school, baptism and marriage records, we have been able to find many of the first names and build more of a picture of the families and their occupations.

The position of 'out-workers' is less clear. These were usually women who would collect work from the factories and complete it in their living rooms and kitchens. (A practice known locally as 'felling'). Many of them would have been in families involved in the strike and are likely therefore to have supported it even if they weren't union members themselves.

The NUBSO membership lists were split into male and female members. We've listed the members jointly for ease of publication and to show possible family connections. (However, the same surname doesn't necessarily indicate one family, as there are different families sharing the same name.) It's worth noting that some families had relations who were on 'the other side' of the dispute.

The list is of local women and men who joined the union between 1918 and 1922, and whom we believe were involved in the strike, and/ or the co-operative factory. We've added first names we think are correct. Where we've been unable to verify first names, we've just left the initial. We've also created separate lists for each village, though village boundaries were slightly different in 1918.

The occupations and estimated ages in 1918 are based largely on the 1911 census. Note: Some women joined the union when the co-operative factory was set up.

The word 'riveter' was spelt with both one and two 't's. We have left the spelling as in its original use.

NUBSO Members in Eyam around the time of the strike.

Surname	First Name	Age in 1918	Role/Company	Lived
Askham	Edith	30	Machinist	Water Lane
Askham	Nellie	21	Machinist	
Bacon	A (male)			
Barber	Bertha	18	Worked at Ridgeway Bros,	Audrey Cott's
Barber	Clara	18	Worked at West's	Townhead
Barber	Edmond	12		
Barber	Elsie?	11		
Barber	George Edmond	48	Boot maker, sole cutter	Causeway
Barber	James (Jim)	14		Audrey Cottages
Barber	Maggie?	20		
Barber	Mary Emma	23	Machinist at Ridgeway Bro.	Audrey Cott's
Barber	Nellie	15		Causeway
Barber	Tom	54	Warehouseman at West's.	Little Edge Tn'd
Barber	Thomas	16		Little Edge, Townhead
Barber	William Nelson	45	Rivetting machine operator	Audrey Cott's
Barker	Doris			
Barker	Mrs Emily (nee Maddock)	24	Machinist	Townhead
Barker	Mrs Florence ?	54		
Barnes	Farewell (male)	40	Finisher	Birch Place
Betney	Alfred	15		Curbar
Blackwell	Clara	22	Machinist	Club Row
Blackwell	Frank 33 or Fred 35		Finisher	Causeway
Blackwell	Joseph	28	Ridgeway & Fox ?	
Booker	J H (male)			
Bramwell	Alfred	50	Rivetter	
Bramwell	Charles	46	Boot riveter	Water Lane
Bramwell	E (female)			
Bramwell	Horace	25	Rivetter	Club Row, Rock Square

Bramwell	James	38		
Bramwell	Mabel Annie	18	Slipper machinist	Club Row, Rock Square
Bramwell	John Thomas	38	Boot finisher, Ridgeway & Fox.	Steeple Corner
Bramwell	William	58	Rivetter	Club Row, Rock Square
Brocklehurst	E			
Bullard	Beatrice ?	16	Ridgeway & Fox	Townhead
Bullard	Rose	25	Machinist, Ridgeway & Fox	
Burns	Alice	16		
Burns	Emma ?	27		
Burns	Lily ?	18		
Carter?	Mary			
Cooper	Louise Adelaida	26	Machine hand at West's	
Cooper	William Henry	28	Pressman at West's	Church Vw & Main St
Curtis	Mrs Mary Alice	26	Machinist	Townhead
Daniel	Anne Elizabeth	28	Boot binder	Rock Square
Daniel	Annie ?	16		
Daniel	Ellen ?	28	Machinist	The Edge, Club Row
Daniel	George			
Daniel	G (female)			
Daniel	Harry or Henry	35	Boot repairer	Water Lane
Daniel	Ernest ?	19	West's	
Daniel	William			Club Row
Dawson	Harry	47	Boot finisher, Ridgeway Bro.	Laurel Cottage
Dawson	Mary or Emma ?	44	Boot fitter	Stoney Middleton
Elliott	Benjamin?	15		
Elliott	Bertha Francis ?	15-17		Little Edge
Fletcher	Charles	27	Rivetter	
Fox	Mrs W			
Frith	Annie	17		
Frith	Lilian (Lily)	21	Machinist	
Frith	Lucy or Louisa			
Frith	Nellie ?	14		
Frith	Rachel ?	22		Townhead
Furness	E (could be Emily Mary 40 or Eliza 24 or Elizabeth or Emma 58)			
Furness	Lydia			
Furness	N (female)			
Furness	Victoria Doris ?			
Green	Annie	15		Birch Place
Gregory	Clara ?	17		Townhead
Gregory	Percy	16 or 34		
Gregory	S (male)			
Hall	Elizabeth	44	Slipper binder	Town End & Main St
Hall	Kate			
Hall	Robert J	37	Boot finisher	Main Street
Hallam	Annie or Agnes ?			
Hancock	H (male)			
Hancock	Mrs H			
Harrison	Joseph (Joe)	50	Clicker	Church Street

Higinbotham	Mrs			
Hobson	JW (male)			
Hoskin	S (female)			
Howard	Ivy ?	21		Ball House, Eyam
Jackson	Ada or Alice	33 or 24	Both machinists	
Lowe	Edith Emma ?	21	Machinist	Water Lane
Lowe	Herbert	23	Rivetter	
Lowe	Joseph White	54	Boot maker	
Lowe	Mary Ann ?	21	Machinist	
Lowe	Mrs			
Lowe	William	41	Rivetter	
Loweson	W (male)			
Maddock	Harold	22	Finisher	Townhead
Mason	Kitty			
Mason	Mrs Elizabeth Alice	31	Machinist	
Nettleship	Elsie (or Ethel)	13		Townhead
Nettleship	Lizzie	16		
Nettleship	Nellie	14		Townhead
Purseglove	Bernard	16		
Purseglove	F (male)			
Redfearn	Doris	16		The Cross
Redfearn	Edith	24	Machinist	The Cross
Redfearn	Eric	17		
Redfearn	George	50	Laster	The Cross
Redfern	P (female)			
Richardson	Edward or Ernest	24	Slipper finisher	Townhead
Richardson	Harold			
Ridgeway	George	57	Finisher	Church Street
Robinson	Hannah or Hilda	23 or 31	Machinist	
Robinson	Mrs			
Rowland	Dora	21	Machinist	Rodney House, Town End
Rowland	George	57	Finisher	Town End
Rowland	Gertrude	23	Machinist	Rodney House, Town End
Rowland	Henry	50	Boot finisher	Rodney House, Town End
Slater	Allen	46	Warehouseman	Townhead
Slater	Ann	55 ?		
Slater	Clara	41	Overlooker	Lydgate
Slater	Mary Ann 52 or Mary 17			
Slater	Seth	30	Finisher	Townhead
Slater	Willie or Bill	46	Ridgeway Brothers	Townhead
Smith	D (female)			
Stafford	Walter	52	Machinist	Townhead
Stafford	William	16		
Twigg	Joe	29	Clicker / repairer at West's	
Twigg	Maria?	16		The Causeway
Twigg	Maggie?	23	Machinist	
Twigg	Nora			
Twigg	Thomas	32	Engine driver	Townhead

Udale	Annie	27	Machinist	Thorn
Walton	C (female)			
Ward	Christiana?	16		
Ward	Ruth?	15		
White	Annie	31	Machinist	Church Street
White	Doris?	16		Water Lane
White	George	40	Shoe finisher	Water Lane
White	Maggie or May	34	Machinist	
Whitworth	Grace	26		The Cross
Willis	I (female)			
Willis	M (male)			
Willis	Percy	47	Lasting machinist at West's	Birch Row
Willis	Percy Alwyn	17		
Wilson	Joseph or Jim	30	Sole sewer	Steeple House
Wood	Joseph	31	Machinist	
Wood	Mrs J			

NUBSO Members in Stoney Middleton around the time of the strike.

Surname	**First Name**	**Age in 1918**	**Role/Company**	**Lived**
Baggaley	John	40	(or John Baggaley below)	
Baggaley	John	18		
Baggaley	William	43	Rivetter, Mason & Lennon	The Dale
Baggaley	Wilfred	15		
Bailey	Isaac	41	Rivetter	
Bailey	Mary	30	Boot finisher	
Bailey	Sarah	20		
Barker	George	17	Mason & Lennon	High Street
Barker	Frederick A	24	Rivetter	
Barker	J (male)			
Barker	Mabel	15		
Beebe (Bibby)	Joe	34	Mason & Lennon	Calver
Bennett	Isaac	44	Rivetter, Mason & Lennon	
Brocklehurst	Gerty	16		High Street
Carter	Thomas (Tom)	39	Rivetter, Goddard's	Belmont
Cother	Charles	22	Rivetter	The Dial
Cother	Doris	14		
Cother	Mary	18		The Dial
Cother	Nellie	15		
Dawson	M (female)			
Eidson (Eadson)	Joseph	35		Middleton Dale
Frith	Richard or Ronald	14 or 13		
Gascoyne	W (male)	41		
Hall	George	28	Boot Maker, Heginbotham's	Dale Side
Hancock	Dorothy			
Hancock	Henry	47	Boot Rivetter, Heginbotham's	High Street

Hancock	H or F		Mason & Lennon	
Heginbotham	Joseph	21		
Heginbotham	Frank	40	Boot Rivetter	The Nook
Hodgkinson	George	31	Boot Rivetter	
Jackson	Martha Annie	18		Middleton Bank
Jackson	Marion Elizabeth	12		
Jackson	Stonewall	48	Boot Rivetter	
Jerram	Charles	20		Royal Oak, Stoney
Mason	Edgar or Evelyn	32	Boot Rivetter	
Mason	George	48	Rivetter	The Nook
Mason	John	30	Boot Cutter Out	
Mosley	Beatrice or Barbara	17		
Robinson	Hannah	14		
Robinson	Frank or Fred		Finisher, Mason & Lennon	High Street
Robinson	Jasper	16		High Street
Robinson	Sarah	28	Boot finisher	
Smith	J		Mason & Lennon	
Unwin	William	47		
Unwin	Mrs (no initials given)			
Unwin	George	24	Boot Rivetter	
Wall	Mary Elizabeth	19		
Walton	Clara	25	Boot finisher	
Walton	Frederick	54	Boot Maker / Rivetter	High Street
Ward	David	17		High Street
Ward	George	39	Rough Cutter	High Street
Ward	Mary Elizabeth	18		

Explanatory note

NUBSO continued supporting members who were out of work when the strike ended. However, the Eyam branch of NUBSO had effectively ceased to function by 1923, after the co-operative factory closed. A new local branch of the union was formed in 1941 (during the Second World War), covering workplaces in Stoney Middleton, Eyam and Calver. The membership included a core of workers who'd been involved in the strike and were either at Heginbotham's (the firm which settled with the union), or who had got a job in another local firm.

The new branch was based on workers in the four main companies still operating in the area - Ridgeway and Willis, West's, William Lennon & Co. and Heginbotham's which was now in Calver. These four firms all recognised the union and made agreements based on national wage rates and conditions. The union branch continued after the war.

Officers of the new NUBSO Stoney Middleton branch in the 1940s

The new branch was set up during World War Two (when there was a big demand for boots and shoes), with the help of the NUBSO area organiser at the time, Mr E. Ward.

Branch President: Mr R. Baggaley, Calver
Secretary: Harry Blackwell, Eyam
Committee Members: Mr W.J. Cocker (Heginbotham Brothers), Mr W. Payne (Wm Lennon & Co.), Miss Norah Twigg (Ridgeway & Willis) and Mr Turner (Edmund West)

The local branch of the National Union of General Workers (formerly, the Gas Workers), was prominent in its support for the strikers. Its officers included George Nettleship and J.P. Waterhouse. Significant support for the strikers also came from Sheffield. Prominent figures mentioned in press and union reports included Mr J. Limb (Munitions workers) and Mrs Limb (who organised events to raise money for local children), Mr A. Lockwood, Mr York and a Mr Dobson from Rotherham.

Acknowledgements and thanks

Individuals and groups

Alison Ahern; 100th Anniversary Commemoration group members; Graham Armitage; Trevor Askey; Frances Bagshawe; Linda and Neil Barber;

Tom Barker; Lynn Barker; John Beck; Lois Bekeris; Annette Bindon; Charles Blackwell; David Blackwell; Steve Blackwell; Val Burgess; Cathy Burke; Diana Cameron; Christine Cartledge; Fran and John Clifford; Richard Coates; Mark Cottrell; Ian Cox

Muriel Eades; Eyam – 'Down Memory Lane' Facebook group; Eyam Museum; Eyam Village Society; Jacqueline and Terry Furness; Janet Gilbert; Oona Gilbertson, staff and children at Eyam Primary School; Carole Goodwin; Colin Hall; David Hall; Judith and John Hancock; Jude Hirst; Shirley Holt; Andy Hoult; Eileen Ibbotson; Peter Ibbotson; Frances Jackson; Alan Jacques; Gillian Jinks; Jim & Merlyn Key;

Les Lennon, William Lennon & Co. Ltd; Jill Liddington; Barbara Maltby; Alan McGowan; Geoff Mason; John Mortimer; Marilyn Newton; Mark Noble; Barry Nottage; Leslie Oldfield, Tony Parsons; Dorothy Peel; Joan Plant; Eugenia Ridgeway; Steve Ridgeway; Pat and Derrick Robinson; Tony and Cynthia Robinson; Judith Robinson; Barbara Rollings.

Colin Shaw; Lynette Sidhu; Libs Slattery; Ian Smith; SMILE; Stoney Middleton Heritage Centre Community Group; Stoney Middleton Well Dressing Committee; Stoney Middleton Wesleyan Reform Chapel; Graham Taylor; Ken Thompson; Joel Thompstone; Andrea Tomlinson and Stoney Middleton Primary School; Glenn Trezza; David Turner; Audrey Udale; Kate Upcraft; Joan Watson; Dave Welsh; Merlyn Wiles; Elizabeth Winthrope; River Wolton.

Note: We are also grateful to those who have provided information but wished to remain anonymous.

Staff at the following Libraries, Archives and Museums:

Eyam Museum; Modern Records Centre, University of Warwick Library; Derbyshire Local Studies, Matlock and Chesterfield; Derbyshire Record Office, Matlock; Sheffield Local Studies Library; Imperial War Museum, London; Lancashire Archives, Preston; National Co-operative Archive, Manchester; Leeds Central Library; The British Library, St. Pancras and Boston Spa; The National Archives, Kew; The Working Class Movement

Library, Salford; Marx Memorial Library, London; Northampton Museum & Art Gallery.

Trade Unions

The Community Trade union - especially Bernard at Earl's Barton, NUBSO archives.
GMB, London, especially John Callow; also, Chesterfield, and the archive at the WCML, Salford.

Newspapers and Periodicals

Derby Mercury, Sheffield Daily Telegraph, Derbyshire Courier, Derbyshire Times, High Peak News, Matlock Visitor, Shoe & Leather Record, Boot and Shoe Trade Journal, Labour Gazette (Board of Trade), Leeds Mercury, Yorkshire Evening News, Daily Herald, Derby Daily Telegraph, The Labour Woman, Eyam Parish Magazine.

Main Archives and Primary Sources

NUBSO archives, University of Warwick and 'Community' offices, Earls Barton.
GMB / NUGW archives, Working Class Movement Library, Salford.
Electoral Registers, Eyam and Stoney Middleton 1919 - 23.
Census Reports 1901, 1911, 1921, 1931.
Land Value Map and Schedule, 1910 for Eyam and Stoney Middleton.

With special thanks to Fran Clifford for sharing the results of research on local Marriage, Birth, Burial and School records, and to the Eyam Museum World War One exhibition group.

Online

1911 Census (Ancestry); The British Newspaper Archive; Eyam 'Down Memory Lane' Facebook Group; 'Courage of Conscience' River Wolton (Ed.).
www.smhccg.org.
www.eyam-museum.org.uk (Resources: Eyam Oral Histories, especially George May, Clarice White, Madelaine Cocker, Lily Nettleship, Derek and Paulette Knowles, Alan and Barbara Ashton, Dorothy Fox, Eugenia Ridgeway, Mary O' Connell and Norma Wood).
Graham Stevenson 'Defence or Defiance - A Peoples' History of Derbyshire' Part III
Wishful Thinking *www.places.wishful-thinking.org.uk* .

Books and other publications:

Graham Armitage 'Discover Stoney Middleton' (Stoney Middleton Heritage Centre Community Group 2018).
Bill Bevan (Ed) 'Memories that flow through Calver' (Calver Weir Restoration Project, 2013)
Julie Bunting 'Bygone Industries of the Peak' (Wildtrack Publishing, 2006)
Catherine Burke 'Working Class Politics in Sheffield, 1900 – 1920: A Regional History of the Labour Party' (Ph.D. 1983, Sheffield City Polytechnic)
John Callow 'Freedom's Banner' (GMB 2017)
Tom Carter 'Cobbler's Patches of Memory' (1956, unpublished, courtesy of Christine Cartledge)
Doris Coates 'Tunes on a Penny Whistle' (2nd Edition, Harpsden Press, 2017)
Doris Coates 'Tuppenny Rice & Treacle' (2nd Edition, Harpsden Press, 2017)
George Dangerfield 'The Strange Death of Liberal England' (First published 1935; edition consulted published by Serif, 2013)
Clarence Daniel 'Industries of Eyam' in Derbyshire Miscellany, vol. 1 (1958) and vol. 4 (1967); and 'The History of Eyam' (Loxley Bros. 1932)
Mary Davis (Ed), 'Class and Gender in British Labour History' (Merlin 2011) – especially chapters by Sheila C. Blackburn and Katrina Honeyman on 'sweating'.
Harry Dawson 'Conditions in a Village Boot and Shoe Factory (Up to 1918)' (1974. Unpublished transcript by Doris Coates of notes written by her father; Courtesy of Richard Coates)
Bertram Edwards 'The Burston School Strike' (Lawrence & Wishart, 1974)
Richard van Emden and Stephen Humphries 'All Quiet on the Home Front' – An Oral History of Life in Britain during the First World War (Headline, 2003)
Alan Fox 'A History of the National Union of Boot and Shoe Operatives, 1874 –1957' (Blackwell, 1958)
James Hinton 'The First Shop Stewards' Movement' (George Allen & Unwin 1973)
Yvonne Kapp 'The Air of Freedom – The Birth of the New Unionism' (Lawrence & Wishart, 1989)
Kelly's Directories for Derbyshire 1891- 1941
Jill Liddington 'Rebel Girls' (Virago, 2006)
Geoffrey Mitchell (Ed) 'The Hard Way Up – The Autobiography of Hannah Mitchell' (Virago 1977)
J. T. Murphy 'New Horizons' (John Lane, The Bodley Head, 1941)
National Union of Boot and Shoe Operatives 'Fifty Years' (NUBSO, 1924)
National Union of Boot and Shoe Operatives 'Blowing Our Own Trumpet' (pamphlet and 45rpm record 'Marching Union'. No date but approx. 1960)

E.A. and G.H. Radice 'Will Thorne: Constructive Militant' (George Allen and Unwin, 1974)
Louise Raw 'Striking A Light' (Bloomsbury, 2011)
Chanie Rosenberg '1919' (Bookmarks, 1987)
Sheila Rowbotham 'Hidden from History' (Pluto Press 1990)
Sheila Rowbotham 'Women at War' in 'Armistice 1918-2018' (Observer 2018)
'Stoney Middleton: A Working Village' (SMILE 2002)
June Swann 'Shoemaking' (Shire Publications 1986)
Graham Taylor 'Ada Salter - Pioneer of Ethical Socialism (Lawrence & Wishart, 2016)
Paul Thompson, 'The Edwardians - The Remaking of British Society' (Second ed. Routledge, 1992)
Will Thorne 'My life's battles' (George Newnes, 1925)
Simon Webb '1919, Britain's Year of Revolution' (Pen & Sword, 2016)
Selina Todd 'The People' (John Murray, 2014)

We would like to thank everyone involved in making the 100th anniversary celebrations possible, and all the people who helped to make the exhibitions and assist us with this book. Whilst we have drawn on many sources and spoken to lots of people, we alone remain responsible for the views expressed, interpretation of evidence, and for any mistakes and omissions.

We welcome any comments or new information. Please email either:
Steve Bond (steve.bond@pop3.poptel.org.uk) or:
Phil Taylor (philipjtaylor@live.co.uk).

Phil Taylor and Steve Bond, August 2019.